The
Bible
Atlas

A pictorial guide
to the Holy Lands

Written by Dr. Stephen Motyer

Illustrated by Brian Delf

DK

Dothan●

Shechem●

GILEAD

CANAAN

Bethel●

Gaza●

Hebron●

DEAD
SEA

Beersheba●

●Tanis

GOSHEN

Penguin Random House

REVISED EDITION
Senior Editors Neha Ruth Samuel, Fleur Star
Senior Art Editor Vikas Chauhan
Senior Picture Researcher Nishwan Rasool
US Executive Editor Lori Cates Hand
US Editor Jannah Hankins
Managing Editor Kingshuk Ghoshal
Managing Art Editor Govind Mittal
Senior DTP Designer Harish Aggarwal
DTP Coordinator Vishal Bhatia
Production Editor Jacqueline Street-Elkayam
Senior Production Controller Rachel Ng
Jacket Designer Rhea Menon
Senior Jackets Coordinator Priyanka Sharma Saddi
Jacket Design Development Manager Sophia MTT
Publisher Andrew Macintyre
Associate Publishing Director Liz Wheeler
Art Director Karen Self
Publishing Director Jonathan Metcalf

Consultant Rev. Dr. Andrew Stobart

FIRST EDITION
Project Editor Sadie Smith
Project Art Editor Polly Appleton
Senior Editor Marie Greenwood
Publishing Manager Jayne Parsons
Managing Art Editor Jacquie Gulliver
DTP Designers Andrew O'Brien, Matthew Ibbotson
Picture Research Jo Haddon, Marie Osborn
Jacket Design Dean Price
Production Kate Oliver, Jenny Jacoby
US Editors Claudia Volkman, David Barrett

Additional text by Philip Wilkinson

This American Edition, 2024
First American Edition, 2001
Published in the United States by DK Publishing
1745 Broadway, 20th Floor, New York, NY 10019

Copyright © 2001, 2024 Dorling Kindersley Limited
DK, a Division of Penguin Random House LLC
24 25 26 27 28 10 9 8 7 6 5 4 3 2
002–339170–Feb/2024

A catalog record for this book
is available from the Library of Congress.
ISBN 978-0-7440-9284-4

Printed and bound in UAE

www.dk.com

CONTENTS

4

Discovering the World of the Bible

THE BIBLE IS A COLLECTION of 66 books that tells the story of God's relationship with humans. It is divided into the Old and New Testaments, which contain different kinds of writings such as history, teachings, and poetry. Most of the events in the Bible take place in and around the Holy Land, known at different times as Canaan, the Promised Land, Judah, and Israel. Ancient artifacts and archaeological research reveal the major stories of the Bible in their historical and geographical context.

Fine carving
This ivory carving of a winged, human-headed sphinx is thought to have been made by Phoenician artists. It was found near the ancient Assyrian capital of Nimrud and dates from the 8th or 9th century BCE.

Mosaic from the 6th century CE showing the walled city of Jerusalem

The Bible lands

MOST OF THE EVENTS IN THE BIBLE took place in the region to the east of the Mediterranean Sea, known as the Holy Land. A huge arc of rich farming land, called the Fertile Crescent, stretched all the way from here to Mesopotamia—birthplace of Abraham and the site of some of the world's first major cities, including Ur and Babylon. Further east was Persia (now called Iran). To the southwest of the Holy Land lies Egypt, where a great civilization flourished during Old Testament times. Most people in the Old Testament did not travel outside this area and knew nothing of the world beyond it. By the time of the New Testament, the Holy Land was ruled by the Romans, whose mighty empire stretched from Italy right around the Mediterranean Sea.

MAP OF THE WORLD

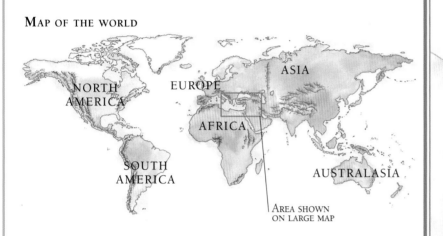

NORTH AMERICA
EUROPE
ASIA
AFRICA
SOUTH AMERICA
AUSTRALASIA

AREA SHOWN ON LARGE MAP

The Judean Desert

The Judean Desert lies to the west of the Dead Sea. It is one of several desert regions in the Bible. Its landscape ranges from craggy chalk hills to low-lying areas near the Dead Sea. The climate is hot, with very little rain and a strong, dry wind. Strange rocky outcrops remain where the winds have worn away the surrounding stone. This is the "Wilderness of Judea" of the New Testament (left).

Mesopotamian marshland

The Tigris and Euphrates are the two great rivers of Mesopotamia. The rivers join north of Basra to form the Shatt-al-Arab (River of the Arabs), which flows into the Persian Gulf. The country here is marshy, with small islands of dry land among streams, canals, and boggy areas. The Israelites were later exiled to this region. These patches of land are now home to the Marsh Arabs. They live by herding water buffalo, and build houses from reeds (right).

(Map showing: Rome, ITALY, Puteoli, MONTENEGRO, ALBANIA, NORTH MACEDONIA, SERBIA, Thessalonica, Berea, GREECE, Rhegium, Syracuse, Corinth, MALTA, MEDITERRANEA, LIBYA)

World of the Bible

The events of the Old Testament took place in the region that is today made up of Israel, Syria, Jordan, Lebanon, Iran, Iraq, and Egypt. Many New Testament stories occurred in the countries to the north and east of the Mediterranean Sea, including Turkey and Greece. On this map the names of towns and cities in the Bible are shown alongside modern country names and borders. Many of the places mentioned in the Bible still exist today.

Farming in the Nile Delta

Ancient Egypt depended entirely on the life-giving waters of the Nile River. Every August the river would rise and flood the land on either side, depositing new rich soil from upstream. The Nile Delta, at the mouth of the river, was formed entirely of this soil and made very fertile farmland.

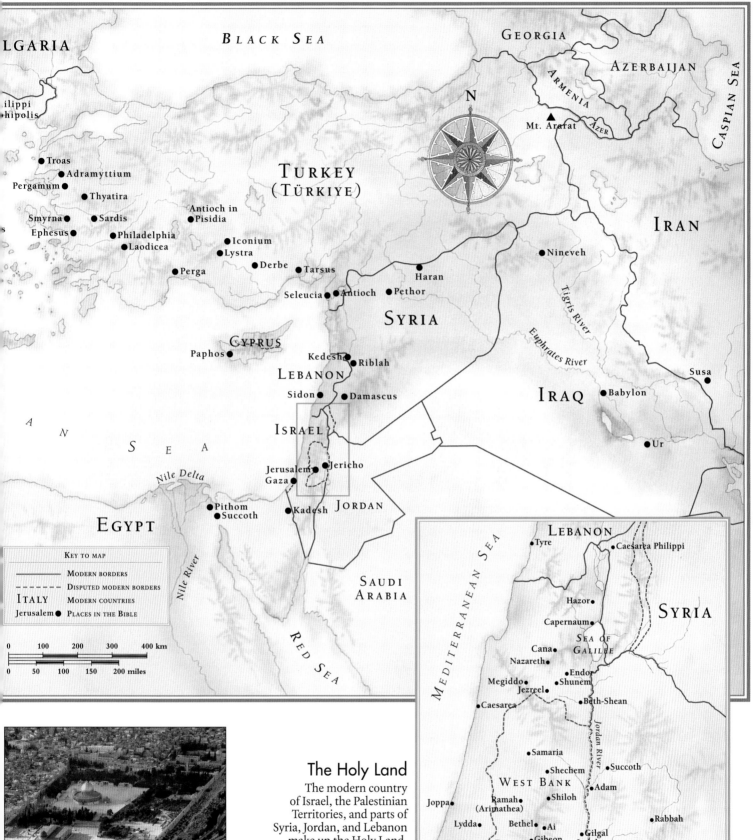

Black Sea

BULGARIA

Philippi
Philipolis

Troas
Adramyttium
Pergamum
Thyatira
Smyrna
Sardis
Ephesus
Philadelphia
Laodicea

GEORGIA

N

AZERBAIJAN

ARMENIA

AZER

CASPIAN SEA

Mt. Ararat

TURKEY
(TÜRKIYE)

IRAN

Antioch in
Pisidia
Iconium
Lystra
Derbe
Perga
Tarsus

Nineveh

Haran

Seleucia Antioch Pethor

SYRIA

Tigris River

CYPRUS

Euphrates River

Paphos

Kedesh
Riblah

LEBANON

Susa

Sidon
Damascus

Babylon

IRAQ

A

N

S

E

A

ISRAEL

Ur

Nile Delta

Jerusalem Jericho
Gaza

EGYPT

Pithom
Succoth

Kadesh

JORDAN

Nile River

SAUDI
ARABIA

RED SEA

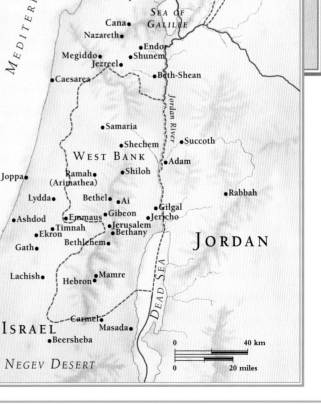

LEBANON

MEDITERRANEAN SEA

Tyre

Caesarea Philippi

Hazor

SYRIA

Capernaum

Cana

Sea of Galilee

Nazareth

Megiddo
Jezreel

Endor
Shunem

Caesarea

Beth-Shean

Jordan River

Samaria

Shechem

Succoth

WEST BANK

Adam

Joppa

Ramah
(Arimathea)

Shiloh

Lydda

Bethel

Ai

Gibeon

Gilgal
Jericho

Rabbah

Ashdod

Emmaus

Timnah

Jerusalem
Bethany

Ekron

Bethlehem

JORDAN

Gath

Lachish

Mamre

Hebron

DEAD SEA

ISRAEL

Carmel

Masada

Beersheba

NEGEV DESERT

0 40 km

0 20 miles

Holy city of Jerusalem

The most important city of Biblical times was Jerusalem. It remains sacred to Jews, Christians, and Muslims. Set high in the hill country of Judah, it became the Israelites' capital city. At the heart of Jerusalem was the sacred Jewish Temple. Only the Western Wall of the Temple courtyard remains.

The Holy Land

The modern country of Israel, the Palestinian Territories, and parts of Syria, Jordan, and Lebanon make up the Holy Land, where God promised to settle Abraham's descendants. This region has varied geography, from the low, flat coast to inland hills where sheep and cattle graze. Further east is the Jordan valley, with its dramatic gorges, and the fish-filled Sea of Galilee. Beyond the Jordan River lies a flat plateau, while to the southwest is the parched Negev Desert.

Mapping the world of the Bible

PEOPLE HAVE BEEN MAKING MAPS of the Bible lands for hundreds of years, but it wasn't until the 19th century that the first geographically accurate maps were made. The geography of this part of the world has always been of great interest to people because of the many important events and journeys that are described in the Bible. Through mapmaking and archaeology, the events of the Bible are made even more vivid. Archaeologists and mapmakers help bring the history of Old and New Testament times to life through studies of the landscape, the objects found, and the ancient sites they discover.

The Jordan River is shown full of fish.

Bethabara, home of John the Baptist.

Two boats can be seen sailing on the Dead Sea.

The Dead Sea Scrolls

In 1947, a Bedouin shepherd boy, wandering near the Dead Sea, threw a stone into the open mouth of a cave above him. He was surprised to hear the sound of breaking pottery. The boy climbed up and found several large jars containing ancient manuscripts. The Dead Sea Scrolls, as they became known, had been hidden in the caves near Qumran during the 1st century CE. The documents provide a rich picture of a variety of religious beliefs and practices during the time of Jesus.

Jericho is depicted as a walled town with many towers.

The Garden of Gethsemane, where Jesus was betrayed

Jerusalem is shown in great detail. (See pages 4–5)

The Dead Sea Scrolls were found rolled up in clay storage jars.

Most of the scrolls were made from leather or papyrus.

A figure kneels to pay tribute.

Black Obelisk

This is one of the carved panels on the side of an Assyrian monument known as the Black Obelisk. It shows King Jehu of Israel, who is introduced in the book of 2 Kings in the Bible, bowing before King Shalmaneser III of Assyria in 841 BCE. The Black Obelisk was discovered at Nimrud in 1846 by archaeologist Henry Layard. It is more than 6 ft (2 m) high, and is now kept in the British Museum in London.

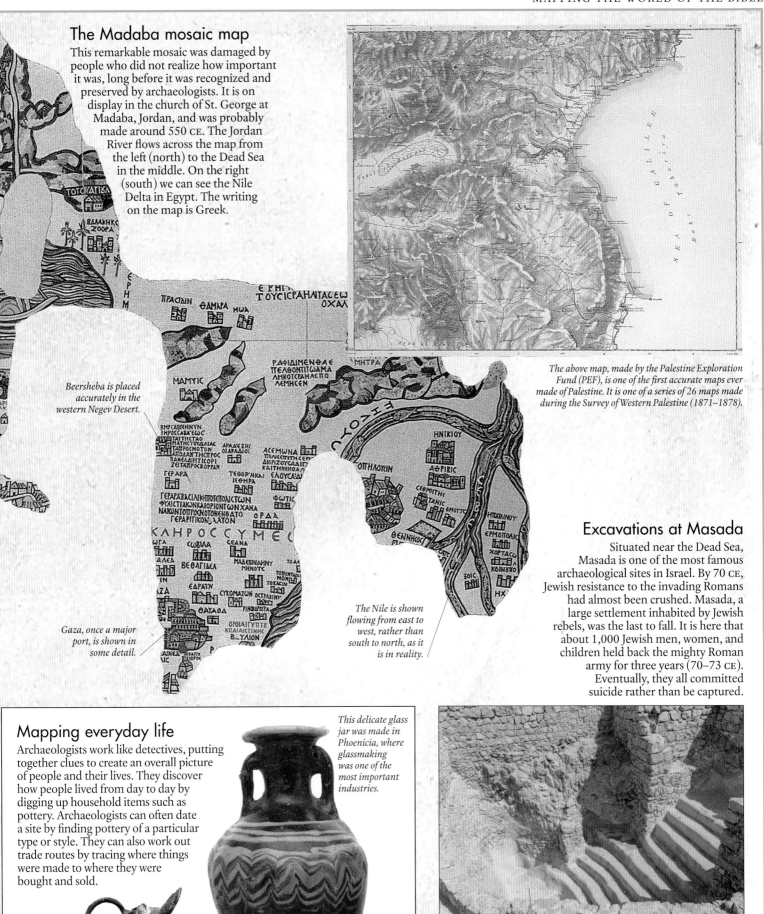

The Madaba mosaic map

This remarkable mosaic was damaged by people who did not realize how important it was, long before it was recognized and preserved by archaeologists. It is on display in the church of St. George at Madaba, Jordan, and was probably made around 550 CE. The Jordan River flows across the map from the left (north) to the Dead Sea in the middle. On the right (south) we can see the Nile Delta in Egypt. The writing on the map is Greek.

Beersheba is placed accurately in the western Negev Desert.

Gaza, once a major port, is shown in some detail.

The Nile is shown flowing from east to west, rather than south to north, as it is in reality.

The above map, made by the Palestine Exploration Fund (PEF), is one of the first accurate maps ever made of Palestine. It is one of a series of 26 maps made during the Survey of Western Palestine (1871–1878).

Excavations at Masada

Situated near the Dead Sea, Masada is one of the most famous archaeological sites in Israel. By 70 CE, Jewish resistance to the invading Romans had almost been crushed. Masada, a large settlement inhabited by Jewish rebels, was the last to fall. It is here that about 1,000 Jewish men, women, and children held back the mighty Roman army for three years (70–73 CE). Eventually, they all committed suicide rather than be captured.

Mapping everyday life

Archaeologists work like detectives, putting together clues to create an overall picture of people and their lives. They discover how people lived from day to day by digging up household items such as pottery. Archaeologists can often date a site by finding pottery of a particular type or style. They can also work out trade routes by tracing where things were made to where they were bought and sold.

This delicate glass jar was made in Phoenicia, where glassmaking was one of the most important industries.

This beautiful jug, made in the shape of a bull, was made in Cyprus and imported to Canaan.

The excavated site of a mikve at Masada. These bathing areas were where the Jewish people performed their purification (washing) ceremonies.

The Old Testament

FROM THE RUGGED MOUNTAINS OF SINAI
to the salty Dead Sea, the events of the
Old Testament took place in some of
the world's most dramatic scenery. On their
journeys through this landscape, the founders
of Israel faced the barren deserts of the Negev,
the thickets and scrub of the Jordan valley, and
the forested hill country of Judah. They also
came into contact with the ancient settlements
of Mesopotamia and Egypt, and the
magnificent city of Babylon. On the way, God
directed them to create their own nation,
centred on the Holy City of Jerusalem.

God's promise to Abraham
The story of the Israelites begins with Abraham. God promised
Abraham that he would become the father of a great nation and that
he would have as many descendants as there are stars in the sky.

*The view from Mount Sinai, in the
Sinai Peninsula in Egypt*

The journeys of the Patriarchs

1. Abraham's descendants
God promised Abraham that he would have as many descendants as there are stars in the sky. Abraham and his wife Sarah were 100 and 90 years old when God finally granted them a child, Isaac.

THE BOOK OF GENESIS describes how Terah embarked on an epic journey with his son Abraham and the rest of his family. They left behind the glittering city of Ur in southern Mesopotamia, and traveled northwest to Haran. The family led a nomadic life, herding their sheep and cattle along the banks of the Euphrates River. Years later, God told Abraham to travel south to the hill country of Canaan, where he would become "the father of a new nation." Abraham found pasture for his flocks around Hebron, and traveled to Egypt through Beersheba. Abraham's son Isaac and Isaac's son Jacob were also travelers. Abraham, Isaac, and Jacob are known as the Patriarchs, the founding fathers of the nation of Israel.

Abraham sacrificed a ram in place of Isaac.

2. Abraham's test
To test Abraham's faith, God ordered Abraham to take Isaac to Moriah (later called Jerusalem) and make the greatest sacrifice of all—to kill his son. Abraham was about to carry out God's wishes when an angel appeared and ordered him to stop. Abraham had proved that he placed his love of God before everything.

MEDITERRANEAN SEA

CANAAN

Haran

Halab

Hamath

Damascus

Hazor

Bethel

Moriah (Jerusalem)

Hebron

Beersheba

Abraham may have followed traders or local nomadic tribes on his journey to Canaan.

Jacob disguised himself as his hairy brother Esau by covering his hands and neck with goatskin.

EGYPT

River Nile

ABRAHAM'S JOURNEY ———
JACOB'S JOURNEY ———

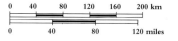

| 0 | 40 | 80 | 120 | 160 | 200 km |
| 0 | | 40 | | 80 | 120 miles |

3. Jacob and Esau
Isaac and his wife Rebekah had twin sons, Jacob and Esau. God promised Rebekah that her favorite son, Jacob, would be Isaac's heir even though Esau was the older brother. So Jacob and his mother tricked Isaac, who was old and blind, into giving Jacob his blessing. When Esau found out, he was furious, and Jacob fled to Haran.

5. Jacob and Rachel
In Haran, Jacob lived with his uncle Laban, a sheep farmer. Jacob fell in love with Laban's beautiful daughter, Rachel, and Laban promised that they could marry if Jacob worked for him for seven years. When the time was up, Laban fooled Jacob into marrying Rachel's older sister, Leah. Laban finally allowed Jacob to marry Rachel, but Jacob had to promise to work for another seven years.

Builders used mud bricks to build distinctive beehive-shaped houses.

The Sumerians are believed to have invented the wheel, which they used when making pots.

The rivers provided a rich source of fish for the Sumerians.

River Tigris

MESOPOTAMIA

Sumerian craftspeople were renowned for the gold jewelry and ornaments they made for the royal family.

Sumerian treasure
This solid gold helmet was buried in the royal graves of Ur. It was just one item among hundreds made of costly materials such as silver, gold, and semi-precious stones. These "grave goods" were intended for the king and queen to use in the next world. They show the fabulous wealth of the rulers in this part of southern Mesopotamia, known as Sumer.

The ziggurat at Ur was a huge mud-brick temple dedicated to Nanna, the Sumerian moon god.

River Euphrates

The Sumerians developed one of the first writing systems. They wrote on damp clay tablets, which dried and set into hardened tablets.

Ur ●

Date palms grew in the salty marshland of Mesopotamia. The Sumerians ate the dates and used the wood to build their homes.

4. Jacob's ladder
On his way to Haran, Jacob dreamed about a staircase stretching to heaven, with angels walking up and down the steps. In the dream, God spoke to Jacob, promising him that the land where he slept would later be his, and that his children would live there. Jacob named the place Bethel, meaning "House of God."

Sumerian merchants sailed along the coasts of the Persian Gulf, trading in gold, ivory, hardwoods, and precious stones.

Tel Be'er Sheva

Archaeologists have unearthed an ancient city at Tel Be'er Sheva near modern-day Beersheba, 48 miles (77 km) southwest of Jerusalem. It may be the site of the Biblical city of Beersheba, where Abraham settled. The tel is a mound made from many layers of settlements. The ruins shown here date from the Iron Age (1000–720 BCE).

The Israelites in Egypt

JACOB AND HIS FAMILY prospered as farmers in Canaan's hill country. Then a terrible famine struck. Jacob and his sons traveled to Egypt in search of food. There they were reunited with Jacob's favorite son, Joseph, who had been sold into slavery in Egypt many years earlier. Joseph had risen to the position of vizier (governor) to Pharaoh, the ruler of Egypt. Pharaoh allowed Jacob's family to settle in the north of his land. This was the delta region, where the great Nile River divided into many separate streams that overflowed into swamps and marshes. The soil was damp and grew rich grass for goats and cattle. Here, over several generations, Jacob's family grew into the twelve tribes of Israel. The Israelites flourished in Goshen and as time passed they forgot their homeland in Canaan.

After buying Joseph as a slave in Dothan, the merchants continued to Egypt.

ROUTE OF SPICE MERCHANTS

GILEAD

CANAAN

Dothan

Shechem

1. How Joseph got to Egypt

When Joseph was 17 years old, Jacob gave him a beautiful coat. This infuriated Joseph's jealous older brothers, who plotted to get rid of Joseph. One day, while looking after their flocks at Dothan in Canaan, the brothers threw Joseph down a well, leaving him for dead. Just then a group of spice merchants from Gilead passed by on their way to Egypt. The brothers dragged Joseph out of the well and sold him as a slave to the traders for twenty pieces of silver. As Joseph was taken to Egypt, the brothers smeared his coat with goat's blood and told Jacob that a wild animal had killed his son.

On the banks of the Nile

The Nile River was Egypt's lifeline. Every year it flooded, spreading rich mud over the land on both banks. This narrow strip of fertile soil was where most of the Egyptian people lived, growing crops such as wheat and barley. Beyond was parched desert and rock-strewn mountains.

Joseph was brought before Pharaoh to explain the Egyptian leader's strange dreams.

2. Joseph interprets Pharaoh's strange dreams

Years later, Pharaoh had two mysterious dreams, in one of which seven thin cows ate up seven fat ones, but grew no fatter. "What could it mean?" wondered Pharaoh. Joseph told Pharaoh that Egypt would enjoy seven good harvests, followed by seven bad years. This prediction, given to Joseph by God, soon came true. Pharaoh made Joseph his vizier, second in command, in charge of storing grain for the years of famine ahead.

DEAD SEA

Hebron ●

Beersheba ●

Gaza ●

Ships were powered by both oars and sails. This allowed them to travel at great speed.

Farmers cut their grain using stone-bladed wooden sickles. The straw was later made into mats and baskets.

3. Joseph meets his brothers

When famine struck Canaan, Joseph's elder brothers travelled to Egypt looking for food. Joseph recognized his brothers immediately, but they did not recognize him. Joseph sold them some grain, but told them to come back with their youngest brother, Benjamin. When they returned, Joseph accused Benjamin of stealing and refused to let him leave with the others. He did this to test his brothers. Knowing how upset Jacob would be to lose another son, one of the brothers, Judah, begged to take Benjamin's place. Joseph realized his brothers had changed. He revealed his identity to them, then sent for Jacob and the rest of his family.

4. Joseph is reunited with his father

Jacob was overjoyed that his favorite son was still alive. After their tearful reunion, they went to see Pharaoh. The Egyptian ruler granted Joseph's people—the Israelites—an area in the land of Goshen, in the eastern Nile Delta. This was some of the best land in all Egypt. Here the Israelites tended their goats and cattle for generations, living peacefully alongside the Egyptians.

Only the most prosperous farmers could afford herds of cattle. Beef was a luxury meat, eaten by wealthy Egyptians.

Tanis ●

GOSHEN

Rameses ●

Bubastis ●

Heliopolis ●

The Step Pyramid at Saqqara, tomb of Pharaoh Djoser, was the first of all the pyramids to be built.

Giza ●

Saqqara ●

Heracleopolis ●

A small, lightweight wooden plough, pulled by a pair of cattle, easily cut through Egypt's sandy soil.

EGYPT

| 0 | 50 | 100 km |
| 0 | 50 | 100 miles |

River Nile

Shadufs were devices for lifting heavy buckets of water from the Nile. Canals carried the water to distant fields, far from the river.

The Great Pyramid at Giza had been standing for hundreds of years by the time the Israelites settled in Egypt.

The Egyptians hunted waterfowl among the reeds of the Nile with boomerang-shaped throw sticks.

Recording the harvest

This colorful Egyptian tomb painting dates from around 1400 BCE. It comes from the tomb of Menna in the important Egyptian city of Thebes. On the right, a group of scribes use reed pens and papyrus to record the harvest. These records informed Pharaoh's officials how much food was available and how much tax they could collect from farmers.

19

The flight from Egypt

LIFE WAS GOOD FOR THE ISRAELITES in the well-watered fields of Goshen. God blessed them, and they grew greatly in number. However, as time passed, the rulers of Egypt saw the Israelites as a threat and enslaved them to work on Egypt's great building projects. Then the Pharaoh commanded that every Israelite boy should be killed at birth. God sent Moses to rescue the Israelites. Moses entered Pharaoh's palace with God's demand, "Let my people go!" But Pharaoh refused. Ten dreadful plagues then struck Egypt, until Pharaoh gave in and ordered the Israelites to leave. Pharaoh's army chased after the fleeing Israelites and nearly trapped them, but God parted the Red Sea, allowing Moses and his people to cross safely to the other side. From there they traveled south to Mount Sinai where God gave Moses the Ten Commandments. The Israelites wandered north across the hot Sinai Desert in the direction of Canaan—the land God had promised Abraham.

Egyptian scribes kept records for Pharaoh. They also wrote stories and acted as secretaries.

1. Moses in the reeds

Jochebed, an Israelite woman, hid her newborn son Moses from Egyptian soldiers for three months. As Moses grew, it became more and more difficult to keep him hidden. Putting her trust in God, Jochebed left her son floating in a papyrus basket on the Nile, near the place where Pharaoh's daughter bathed. The princess rescued the baby—and then unknowingly employed Moses' mother to look after him.

EGYPT

Tanis

Rameses

Bubastis

GOSHEN

Heliopolis

Giza

Nile River

Papyrus reeds grew along the banks of the Nile. The reeds were cut, dried, and woven into sheets to make paper to write on.

Egyptian army chariots could move very quickly into battle. Each chariot had a driver and a soldier. Chariots like these pursued the Israelites to the Red Sea.

2. The burning bush

Moses grew up in Pharaoh's palace. One day he killed an Egyptian slaveholder who was torturing an Israelite. He fled from Egypt to Midian, where he became a shepherd. Years later, wandering with his sheep in the Sinai Desert, Moses saw a bush that was in flames, but not burning up. A voice called out: "Moses! Take off your shoes—this is holy ground." It was God. He sent Moses back to Egypt to rescue the Israelites.

3. Crossing the Red Sea

When the Israelites left Egypt, Pharaoh immediately regretted letting them go, and sent his army to bring them back. The army caught up with the Israelites at the Red Sea. Trapped between the army and the water, the Israelites were terrified. But Moses held out his staff, and to the Israelites' amazement, God parted the water and they crossed the sea on dry ground.

The plagues of Egypt

Moses and his brother Aaron went to Pharaoh to ask for freedom for the Israelites. When Pharaoh refused to let them leave Egypt, ten plagues struck the country. Each plague was worse than the last but Pharaoh would not give in. Finally, God told Moses that every firstborn child and animal in Egypt would die. However, the Israelites would be spared this terrible plague if they followed God's instructions. They had to smear lamb's blood over their doorposts so God would know to pass over their homes. At midnight, this devastating plague struck and at last Pharaoh ordered the Israelites to leave.

The waters of the Nile turned to blood.

Frogs infested the Egyptians' homes.

Huge swarms of gnats appeared.

Millions of flies invaded

All the livestock in Egypt suddenly died.

Boils broke out on people's skin.

Hail rained down, destroying the crops.

Locusts stripped the land of vegetation.

Darkness fell over Egypt for three days.

Israelites survived the plague of the firstborn.

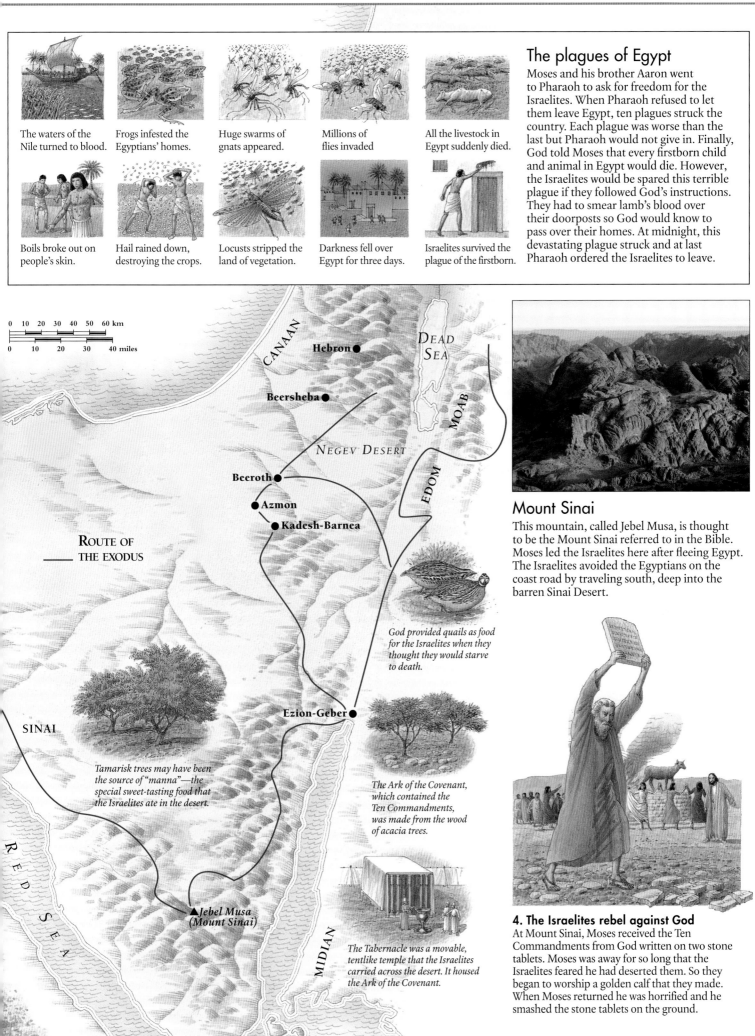

0 10 20 30 40 50 60 km
0 10 20 30 40 miles

CANAAN

Hebron

DEAD SEA

MOAB

Beersheba

NEGEV DESERT

EDOM

Beeroth

Azmon

Kadesh-Barnea

ROUTE OF THE EXODUS

God provided quails as food for the Israelites when they thought they would starve to death.

SINAI

Tamarisk trees may have been the source of "manna"—the special sweet-tasting food that the Israelites ate in the desert.

Ezion-Geber

The Ark of the Covenant, which contained the Ten Commandments, was made from the wood of acacia trees.

RED SEA

▲Jebel Musa (Mount Sinai)

MIDIAN

The Tabernacle was a movable, tentlike temple that the Israelites carried across the desert. It housed the Ark of the Covenant.

Mount Sinai

This mountain, called Jebel Musa, is thought to be the Mount Sinai referred to in the Bible. Moses led the Israelites here after fleeing Egypt. The Israelites avoided the Egyptians on the coast road by traveling south, deep into the barren Sinai Desert.

4. The Israelites rebel against God

At Mount Sinai, Moses received the Ten Commandments from God written on two stone tablets. Moses was away for so long that the Israelites feared he had deserted them. So they began to worship a golden calf that they made. When Moses returned he was horrified and he smashed the stone tablets on the ground.

The Promised Land

WHEN AT LAST THE ISRAELITES reached the border of the Promised Land (Canaan), they realized what a huge task lay ahead. The Canaanites, who lived there already, were powerful and their cities were strongly fortified. Just as the Israelites were about to cross the border, Moses died. His successor, Joshua, led the Israelites across the Jordan River near Jericho and into Canaan. The river miraculously dried up, allowing the Israelites to cross—a sign that God was with them. One by one, the great Canaanite cities began to fall before the Israelite armies, starting with the mighty city of Jericho. After Joshua's victories, many Canaanites remained in the land, but they could not stop Joshua from dividing it among the twelve tribes of Israel. Eventually the Israelites settled in the land that God had promised to Abraham centuries earlier.

The campaigns of Joshua

Joshua was a brilliant military commander, and God was with him. In his first campaign he conquered the mountainous southern part of Canaan, defeating the kings of Jerusalem, Hebron, Lachish, and Eglon at Makkedah. Then he moved north, where he defeated the combined armies of Hazor, Madon, Achshaph, and Shimron.

NORTHERN CAMPAIGN
SOUTHERN CAMPAIGN

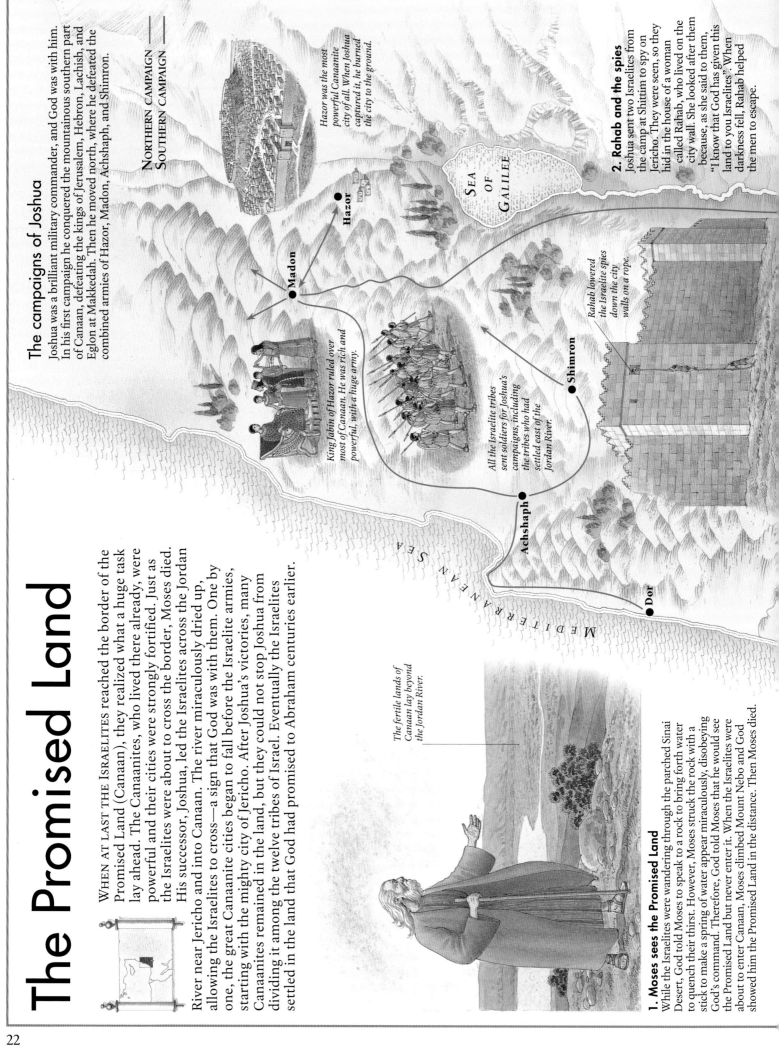

Hazor was the most powerful Canaanite city of all. When Joshua captured it, he burned the city to the ground.

SEA OF GALILEE

Hazor

Madon

King Jabin of Hazor ruled over most of Canaan. He was rich and powerful, with a huge army.

All the Israelite tribes sent soldiers for Joshua's campaigns, including the tribes who had settled east of the Jordan River.

Achshaph

Shimron

Dor

MEDITERRANEAN SEA

Rahab lowered the Israelite spies down the city walls on a rope.

2. Rahab and the spies

Joshua sent two Israelites from the camp at Shittim to spy on Jericho. They were seen, so they hid in the house of a woman called Rahab, who lived on the city wall. She looked after them because, as she said to them, "I know that God has given this land to you Israelites." When darkness fell, Rahab helped the men to escape.

The fertile lands of Canaan lay beyond the Jordan River.

1. Moses sees the Promised Land

While the Israelites were wandering through the parched Sinai Desert, God told Moses to speak to a rock to bring forth water to quench their thirst. However, Moses struck the rock with a stick to make a spring of water appear miraculously, disobeying God's command. Therefore, God told Moses that he would see the Promised Land but never enter it. When the Israelites were about to enter Canaan, Moses climbed Mount Nebo and God showed him the Promised Land in the distance. Then Moses died.

The Ark of the Covenant

The Jordan River flows from the north into the Dead Sea. At 1,365 ft (416 m) below sea level, it is the lowest river on Earth.

▲ *Mount Nebo*

Jordan River

Shittim

Gilgal

Jericho

DEAD SEA

Ai

Gideon

Jerusalem

Bethlehem

Beth-Shemesh

Makkedah

Hebron

Lachish

Debir

Eglon

The Canaanites lived in close family groups. They kept sheep and cattle, and were skilled potters and metalworkers.

At first, the Israelites were defeated at Ai because some of them had stolen gold and silver from Jericho, against God's instructions. The culprits were dealt with, and then Joshua captured Ai.

20 km

15

10 miles

10

5

5

0

0

3. The fall of Jericho

At God's instructions, seven priests, walking in front of the Ark and holding trumpets made from rams' horns, marched once around the city walls of Jericho. They did this every day for six days. On the seventh day, the priests marched around the city seven times, and then blew the rams' horns as loudly as they could. The walls came crashing to the ground. Only Rahab and her family survived.

The Israelites stormed Jericho when the walls began to crumble. They captured the city easily.

The Twelve Tribes of Israel

This map shows where the tribes of Israel settled in their new land. Each tribe is represented by a symbol. The tribe of Levi had no land of its own. Instead, the Levites were priests who lived across the whole land.

Asher

Naphtali

Zebulun

Issachar

Manasseh

Gad

Ephraim

Reuben

Dan

Benjamin

Judah

Simeon

Israel and the Philistines

A FEW YEARS AFTER the Israelites settled in the Promised Land more invaders arrived, this time from the sea. The most famous—the Philistines—settled in an area that the Israelites had not occupied and centered on the five cities of Ashdod, Ekron, Ashkelon, Gath, and Gaza. For the next six hundred years, the Philistines were enemies of the Israelites. After the Israelite leader Joshua, the Israelites were ruled by a series of judges. One of the greatest judges, Samson, won many great battles against the Philistines, but eventually the Israelites decided that they needed a king to help them defeat the Philistines. So the last judge, Samuel, anointed Saul as the first king of the Israelites. When Saul disobeyed God, God chose David to be king instead. David had already won a famous victory over the Philistines by killing their hero, Goliath.

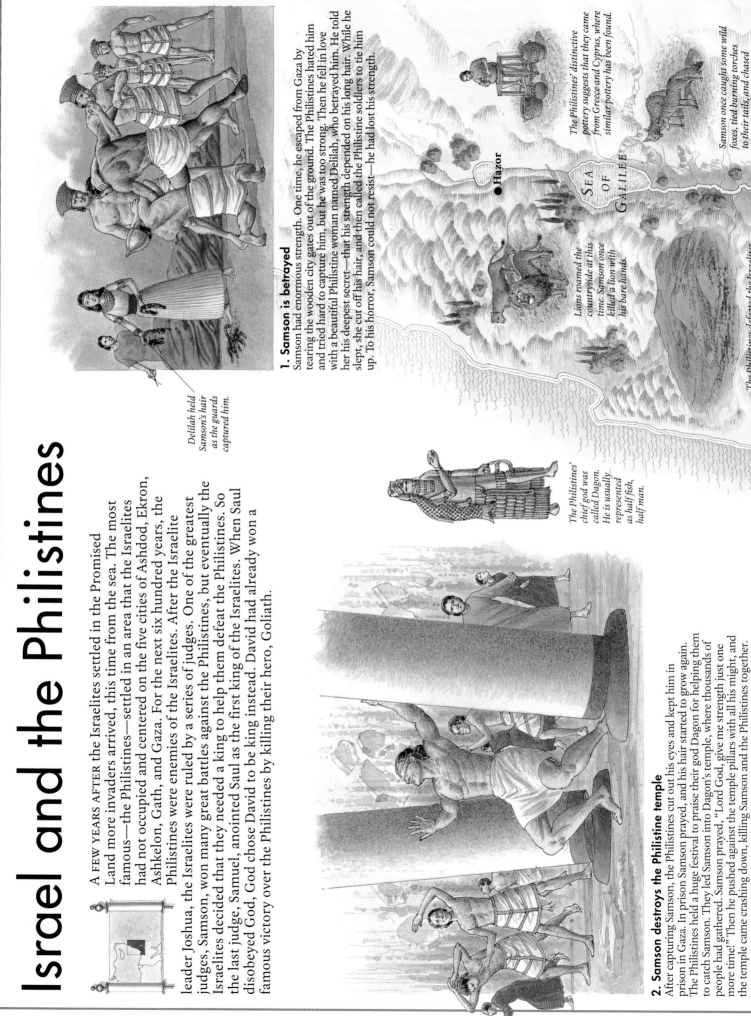

Delilah held Samson's hair as the guards captured him.

1. Samson is betrayed

Samson had enormous strength. One time, he escaped from Gaza by tearing the wooden city gates out of the ground. The Philistines hated him and tried hard to capture him, but he was too strong. Then he fell in love with a beautiful Philistine woman named Delilah, who betrayed him. He told her his deepest secret—that his strength depended on his long hair. While he slept, she cut off his hair, and then called the Philistine soldiers to tie him up. To his horror, Samson could not resist—he had lost his strength.

The Philistines' distinctive pottery suggests that they came from Greece and Cyprus, where similar pottery has been found.

Samson once caught some wild foxes, tied burning torches to their tails, and chased them into the Philistines' fields at harvest time.

• Hazor

SEA OF GALILEE

Lions roamed the countryside at this time. Samson once killed a lion with his bare hands.

The Philistines defeated the Israelites on Mount Gilboa, deep in Israelite

The Philistines' chief god was called Dagon. He is usually represented as half fish, half man.

2. Samson destroys the Philistine temple

After capturing Samson, the Philistines cut out his eyes and kept him in prison in Gaza. In prison Samson prayed, and his hair started to grow again. The Philistines held a huge festival to praise their god Dagon for helping them to catch Samson. They led Samson into Dagon's temple, where thousands of people had gathered. Samson prayed, "Lord God, give me strength just one more time!" Then he pushed against the temple pillars with all his might, and the temple came crashing down, killing Samson and the Philistines together.

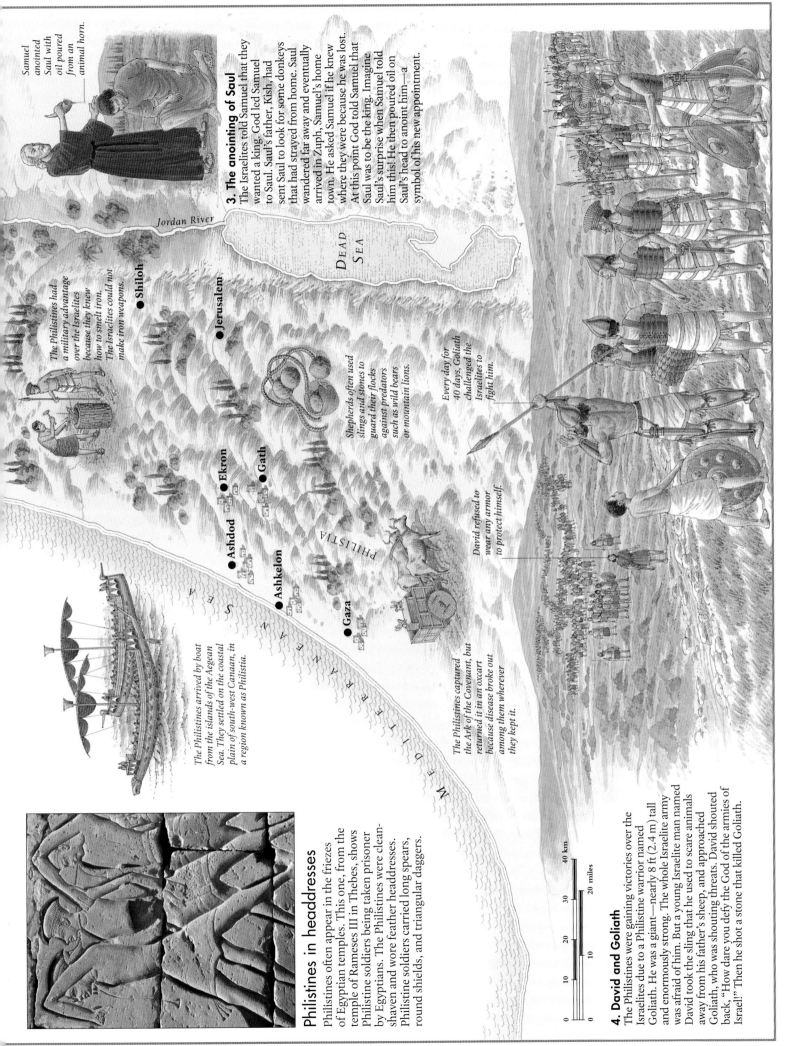

Samuel anointed Saul with oil poured from an animal horn.

3. The anointing of Saul

The Israelites told Samuel that they wanted a king. God led Samuel to Saul. Saul's father, Kish, had sent Saul to look for some donkeys that had strayed from home. Saul wandered far away and eventually arrived in Zuph, Samuel's home town. He asked Samuel if he knew where they were because he was lost. At this point God told Samuel that Saul was to be the king. Imagine Saul's surprise when Samuel told him this! He then poured oil on Saul's head to anoint him—a symbol of his new appointment.

Jordan River

DEAD SEA

The Philistines had a military advantage over the Israelites because they knew how to smelt iron. The Israelites could not make iron weapons.

● Shiloh

● Jerusalem

● Ekron

● Gath

● Ashdod

● Ashkelon

● Gaza

PHILISTIA

Shepherds often used slings and stones to guard their flocks against predators such as wild bears or mountain lions.

The Philistines arrived by boat from the islands of the Aegean Sea. They settled on the coastal plain of south-west Canaan, in a region known as Philistia.

The Philistines captured the Ark of the Covenant, but returned it in an oxcart because disease broke out among them wherever they kept it.

MEDITERRANEAN SEA

Every day for 40 days, Goliath challenged the Israelites to fight him.

David refused to wear any armor to protect himself.

Philistines in headdresses

Philistines often appear in the friezes of Egyptian temples. This one, from the temple of Rameses III in Thebes, shows Philistine soldiers being taken prisoner by Egyptians. The Philistines were clean-shaven and wore feather headdresses. Philistine soldiers carried long spears, round shields, and triangular daggers.

40 km

30

20

10

0

20 miles

10

4. David and Goliath

The Philistines were gaining victories over the Israelites due to a Philistine warrior named Goliath. He was a giant—nearly 8 ft (2.4 m) tall and enormously strong. The whole Israelite army was afraid of him. But a young Israelite man named David took the sling that he used to scare animals away from his father's sheep, and approached Goliath, who was shouting threats. David shouted back, "How dare you defy the God of the armies of Israel!" Then he shot a stone that killed Goliath.

David's kingdom

WHEN SAUL DIED, the people of Judah made David their king in Hebron, while Saul's son, Ishbosheth, ruled the northern tribes from Mahanaim. Ishbosheth was cruelly murdered, and his tribes asked David to become their king, too. To show this new unity, David made Jerusalem the new capital city of the whole land. The date was just before 1000 BCE. David's power grew rapidly and he led Israel's armies in many great victories over the Philistines. Other fierce neighbors—the Moabites, the Edomites, the Ammonites, and even the Syrians—also submitted to his rule and began paying taxes to Israel. For 40 years David ruled well and God promised him that one of his descendants would always be king in Jerusalem.

1. Bringing the Ark to Jerusalem

As soon as he became king, David held a great festival to bring the Ark of the Covenant into Jerusalem. He wanted to thank God for protecting and supporting him. People came from all over the land to join in the celebrations. There was dancing and singing, music and feasting, and a huge procession led by David, who danced as the Ark entered the city. Everyone was delighted with their new king.

The Ark of the Covenant

EGYPT

River Nile

River Nile

David and his music

David was an expert musician. After he killed Goliath, King Saul employed him to play the lyre and sing. Whenever Saul was troubled, David's music would cheer him up. Later, when David himself was king, his songs became famous. David always sang about God and about God's love for his people. These songs are known as "Psalms".

Medieval Psalter

A "Psalter" is the name for a book containing the Psalms. This beautiful Psalter was made by hand in the 14th century. The page shows Psalm 101, one of many Psalms written by David.

The Lord is my shepherd

In the much-loved Psalm 23, David remembers how he cared for his sheep in Bethlehem, and then pictures himself as a sheep in God's flock, being cared for by God himself. "The Lord is my shepherd, I shall not want. He makes me lie down in green pastures; he leads me beside still waters; he restores my soul. He leads me in right paths for his name's sake." (Psalm 23:1–3)

2. David and Bathsheba

Despite being a good ruler, David had his weaknesses. One day, when he was walking on the roof of his palace, David saw a beautiful woman named Bathsheba bathing nearby. Though she was married to Uriah, one of his soldiers, David ordered Bathsheba to be brought to him. Bathsheba became pregnant with his child. Then David had her husband killed so that he could marry Bathsheba.

David's army was large and well equipped. It was drawn from all the tribes of Israel.

David lived at the beginning of the Iron Age (1000–500 BCE), so his metalworkers were able to make the latest iron weapons for his army.

3. Nathan's story to David

God sent the prophet Nathan to speak to David about Bathsheba and Uriah. "O King, help!" said Nathan. "A rich man has stolen a lamb from his poor neighbor!" David was furious about this injustice. But then Nathan thundered, "You are that man! You have stolen another man's wife, and had him killed!" David felt deeply sorry. Nathan warned him that there would be trouble in his family as a result of his wrongdoing.

Fig trees were cultivated to provide nourishing fruits that could be dried and stored.

Water has always been very precious in Israel's hot climate. Women carried water from the well of Gihon, just outside Jerusalem.

During David's reign, envoys from other countries brought gifts to express submission to their powerful neighbor.

People used stone for building palaces, temples, and protective walls around cities. Houses were usually made from mud bricks.

SYRIA

● Damascus

ARAM

MEDITERRANEAN SEA

● Tyre

Dan ●

Hazor ●

Endor ●

Megiddo ●

Jabesh-Gilead ●

ISRAEL

Shechem ● Mahanaim ●

Shiloh ●

Joppa ●

Jordan River

AMMON

Rabbah ●

Gibeon ● Gilgal ●

Jerusalem ●

Bethlehem ●

Hebron ● En Gedi ●

PHILISTIA

JUDAH

MOAB

EDOM

4. Absalom's rebellion

Some years later, David's son Absalom rebelled against his father, and persuaded many Israelites to follow him. David had to flee Jerusalem, where Absalom had proclaimed himself king. War followed and as Absalom rode off on a mule, his head got caught in the branches of a tree. David's soldiers found him trapped in the tree and put him to death. David returned to Jerusalem, deeply saddened by the death of his rebellious son.

0	20	40	160 km
0	10	80	30	40 miles

City of David

Archaeologists have unearthed this "Stepped Stone Structure" (shown behind the ruins of a house), which may be the supporting wall of King David's palace. It is in an area south of the present-day Old City of Jerusalem, known as the City of David, which was the center of the biblical settlement of Jerusalem. Three thousand years ago, David captured this city from the Canaanites, and he and his son Solomon built new fortifications to make it a strong capital for the kingdom of Israel.

Solomon's Temple

SOLOMON BECAME KING OF ISRAEL when his father, David, died in about 970 BCE. Solomon inherited a large kingdom, with taxes pouring in from many surrounding lands. He became very rich, built a huge palace for himself in Jerusalem, and had many servants and many wives. He divided Israel into 12 districts—each district had to provide food for Solomon's huge household for one month each year. Solomon was also a clever businessman. He bought horses from Egypt and then sold them to traders from other countries. He also imported gold, parrots, spices, and perfume. Solomon married the daughter of the Egyptian pharaoh and built a palace for her. However, his biggest project was the building of a magnificent temple, where all the Israelites could come to worship God.

Cedar transported by sea

This Assyrian stone carving shows ships similar to the ones Solomon used to bring cedar from Tyre. Hiram, the king of Tyre, was Solomon's ally, and provided all the wood and much of the gold for Solomon's Temple.

King Solomon's mines

"Solomon's Pillars" are columns of rock located near some ancient copper mines in the desert south of Jerusalem. They are named after Solomon because he mined precious metals for his great buildings.

Copper ore was dug out of the ground and heated until the metal melted and collected at the bottom of the furnace.

Western Gate

Citadel

Citadel wall

Water Gate

Long caravans of camels arrived at Jerusalem, bringing precious wood and spices from the East.

City wall

The Queen of Sheba

Rumors of Solomon's wealth and wisdom spread far and wide. The Queen of Sheba arrived from her distant kingdom, probably in Ethiopia or present-day Yemen, in order to meet this famous king. She asked Solomon difficult questions, and he answered them wisely. The queen visited the Temple and Solomon's palace and throne room. She saw his servants and soldiers in their rich uniforms, and met his many wives living in luxury. Then she said to Solomon, "It is all much greater than everything I heard! Blessed be the Lord your God, who has delighted in you."

The city of Jerusalem

Like King David, Solomon continued to extend and strengthen the walls around Jerusalem. The city grew in wealth and beauty. In the book of 1 Kings, it says "And the king made silver as common in Jerusalem as stones."

King David had chosen the location for the Temple—the Temple Mount— before he died. It was built on Mount Moriah, north of the city of Jerusalem, and was believed to be the place where Abraham had nearly sacrificed Isaac.

Solomon's wisdom

When Solomon became king, he asked God for the gift of wisdom, so that he could rule well. One day, two women came to Solomon with a baby and both claimed they were its mother. To settle the dispute, Solomon ordered a soldier to cut the baby in two with a sword, and give each mother half. The false mother agreed to this, but the real mother cried, begging Solomon to give the baby to the lying woman rather than kill it. Solomon gave the baby to the mother who cried—he knew that the true mother would not want her baby to be killed.

Palace

The Holy of Holies—the room in which the Ark of the Covenant was kept

A chamber called "The Holy Place"

Solomon used many horses, not just for his army, but also to transport building materials to the Temple site.

Boaz

Altar

Cherubim either side of the Ark

Storerooms

Jachin

The "sea"

Solomon's Temple

It took seven years and thousands of skilled workers to build the magnificent Temple. In front of it stood two huge bronze pillars named Jachin and Boaz, which mean "secure" and "strong". Inside, the walls were covered with cedar and decorated with gold flowers. In the inner sanctuary, huge cherubim (winged angels) stood over the Ark. Outside were storerooms for all the golden lamps, pans, and dishes used by the priests. In the courtyard stood a huge bronze "sea" full of water, which was used for purification rituals, and an altar where sacrifices were offered.

The Western Wall

Solomon's Temple was destroyed by the Babylonians in 586 BCE. The construction of a Second Temple was started 70 years later, which was enlarged and beautified by King Herod during the 1st century CE. Only a few years after Herod's work was completed, the Second Temple was destroyed by the Romans in 70 CE. The only visible part that stands today is the Western Wall, which was one of the retaining walls of the Temple Mount. This is a holy site in Judaism and Jews come from all over the world to pray here.

The Divided Kingdom and foreign invasion

WHEN SOLOMON DIED, his son Rehoboam became king. Rehoboam treated the people so badly, ten of the tribes of Israel broke away from him and followed a different king named Jeroboam. As a result, the kingdom divided into two: Israel in the north, led by Jeroboam, and Judah in the south, led by Rehoboam. The northern tribes of Israel were now cut off from the holy city of Jerusalem, and began to worship other local gods, such as Baal, instead of the god of their ancestors. God sent prophets, such as Elijah in the 9th century BCE, to warn the Israelites of disaster because of their failure to love and worship him. Because the kingdom was divided, it was also very weak. In 724 BCE, a huge Assyrian army invaded the northern kingdom. Many people were killed or taken to Assyria.

1. King Ahaz
The southern kingdom of Judah lived in fear of invasion. Egyptian Pharaoh Shishak I invaded in the 10th century BCE, taking all the treasure. When Ahaz, king of Judah, was defeated by forces from Damascus two centuries later, he thought that their gods must be more powerful than the God of Israel. He shut the Temple and instructed everyone to worship those gods, thinking it would save them from the even mightier Assyrians.

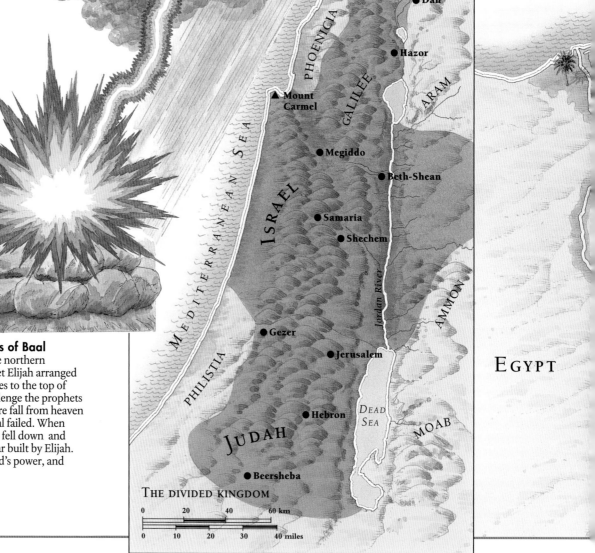

2. Elijah against the prophets of Baal
In order to bring the people of the northern kingdom back to God, the prophet Elijah arranged a contest. He called all the Israelites to the top of Mount Carmel to watch him challenge the prophets of Baal to ask their god to make fire fall from heaven onto an altar. The prophets of Baal failed. When Elijah prayed to the true God, fire fell down and burned up the sacrifice on the altar built by Elijah. The Israelites were amazed by God's power, and returned to worshipping him.

Map labels:
Dan
Hazor
PHOENICIA
GALILEE
ARAM
Mount Carmel
Megiddo
Beth-Shean
MEDITERRANEAN SEA
ISRAEL
Samaria
Shechem
Jordan River
AMMON
Gezer
Jerusalem
EGYPT
PHILISTIA
Hebron
DEAD SEA
MOAB
JUDAH
Beersheba

THE DIVIDED KINGDOM

0   20   40   60 km
0   10   20   30   40 miles

All the kingdoms surrounding the mighty Assyrians had to pay them large amounts of money, called "tributes." If a kingdom refused, the army would take the tribute by force.

The fearsome Assyrian soldiers were well armed and fought fiercely.

Many trading boats brought rich goods to the Assyrians, just as they once did for Solomon.

Israelites were forbidden from making idols, but other peoples often kept statues of their favorite gods in their homes.

The palace at Nimrud had luxurious rooms with magnificent wall carvings and paintings. Nimrud was Assyria's second city, after Nineveh, the capital.

Ivory was skilfully carved to decorate the palaces and temples in Nineveh.

THE ASSYRIAN EMPIRE

Sidon
Tyre
Damascus
ISRAEL
Samaria
Jerusalem
JUDAH
Euphrates River
Nineveh
Nimrud
Tigris River
Babylon
ARABIAN DESERT
PERSIAN GULF
RED SEA
Thebes

3. Jonah and the big fish

God asked Jonah the prophet to go to Nineveh, the capital of the mighty Assyrian Empire, to warn the people there that they would be punished unless they changed their wicked ways. Jonah refused and ran away to the sea—he wanted God to punish the people who had done so much harm to the Israelites. A storm hit at sea and Jonah knew it was because of him. He instructed the sailors to throw him overboard. God sent a huge fish to swallow Jonah. Inside the fish Jonah prayed, and the Lord commanded the fish to spit him out onto dry land. God asked Jonah a second time to preach to the people of Nineveh. This time, Jonah obeyed.

4. The fall of Israel

God became angry with the people of Israel. They had followed the religious practices of other nations, worshipping idols (carved images of gods) and even sacrificing children, despite being warned by God's prophets. In 721 BCE, the Assyrians captured the capital city, Samaria. The northern kingdom of Israel ceased to exist. Its people were captured and sent to live in towns across Assyria, while people from Assyria settled in Israel. But when the new Assyrian settlers refused to worship God, he sent fierce lions to attack them.

| 0 | 100 | 200 | 300 km |
| 0 | 50 | 100 | 150 | 200 miles |

Babylon

THE CITY OF BABYLON was a splendid sight. The towering temple of the god Marduk and the magnificent royal palace were among the most impressive buildings in the ancient world. Babylon owed its wealth to its excellent trading position on the banks of the Euphrates River. The city grew especially powerful under King Nebuchadnezzar II, who reigned from 604 to 562 BCE. He strengthened the city walls, making them wide enough for a four-horse chariot to ride along the top, and constructed the famous Processional Way through the city. It was during this period that Babylon became important in the story of the Jews. Nebuchadnezzar conquered Jerusalem, and thousands of its inhabitants were forced into exile in Babylon. This included Ezekiel, who God called to be his prophet during one of Israel's darkest times.

The wise men of Babylon studied the planets and stars to predict the future.

The Babylonian world

This ancient clay tablet is the only surviving Babylonian world map. It shows how the Babylonians saw the world. Their known world is shown as a circle with the "salt sea" around the edge and Babylon at the center.

Babylon

Aleppo ●

Ebla ●

MEDITERRANEAN SEA

Damascus ●

● Tyre

● Jerusalem

DEAD SEA

Jerusalem's inhabitants were forced to march to Babylon by their captors.

1. The fall of Jerusalem

The book of 2 Kings tells how, in 598 BCE, Nebuchadnezzar besieged Jerusalem and seized the treasures from the Temple and the royal palace. Many Jews, including Jehoiachin, the king of Judah, were taken captive. Nebuchadnezzar appointed Jehoiachin's uncle Zedekiah to rule Jerusalem, but after a few years Zedekiah rebelled. Nebuchadnezzar besieged Jerusalem again. After two years Zedekiah and his people were starving to death, but when they tried to escape, the Babylonians captured them and destroyed the city. Zedekiah was blinded and dragged off to Babylon with the rest of the Jews.

The fiery furnace

Among the exiled Jews in Babylon were three friends—Shadrach, Meshach, and Abednego—who refused to worship the golden statue of Nebuchadnezzar, so he threw them into a blazing furnace. To his amazement, the men walked about unharmed by the flames, accompanied by an angel. The king released the men and allowed them to worship God as they wished.

2. The writing on the wall

King Belshazzar, a successor of Nebuchadnezzar, held a lavish banquet in the royal palace in Babylon. During the feast, the guests drank from golden cups stolen from the Temple in Jerusalem. Suddenly a mysterious hand appeared and wrote a strange message on the wall. Belshazzar was frightened. His wise men could not understand the writing. The queen told Belshazzar to call for the Jewish exile Daniel, who had interpreted Nebuchadnezzar's dreams. Daniel explained that because Belshazzar did not honor God, God would divide his kingdom between the Medes and Persians.

Metalworkers made objects from bronze by pouring hot, molten metal into open molds.

● **Nineveh**

The Babylonians wrote on clay tablets, which they stored in "tablet houses."

Leatherworkers used animal skins to make bags, bottles, harnesses, shoes, and even small boats.

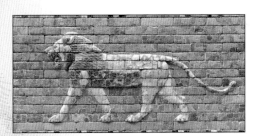

Ishtar lion

This ceramic lion was set into the walls that lined Babylon's great Processional Way. The lion was the symbol of Ishtar, one of the most important of the many Babylonian gods and goddesses. She was their goddess of fertility and war.

The largest of the city's entrances was the Ishtar Gate. It opened on to the Processional Way, a magnificent route through the center of the city.

THE BABYLONIAN EMPIRE

● **Babylon**

● **Nippur**

● **Lagash**

● **Uruk**

Ur ●

The beautiful Hanging Gardens were one of the seven wonders of the ancient world. It is thought that they were built on stepped terraces, with streams trickling down to water the plants.

PERSIAN GULF

Nebuchadnezzar built a colossal golden statue of himself on the open plain of Dura, near Babylon.

3. Daniel in the lions' den

After Babylon's fall to the Medes, King Darius the Mede made Daniel the city's chief administrator. The other administrators were jealous and plotted against Daniel. They persuaded Darius to make a new law, forbidding people to pray to anyone except the king—anyone who refused would be fed to the lions. When the officials caught Daniel praying to God, Darius reluctantly sent Daniel into the lions' den. However, God sent an angel to close the lions' mouths and Daniel's life was spared.

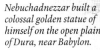

| 0 | 50 | 100 | 150 | 200 km |

| 0 | 50 | 100 miles |

The Tower of Babel

The book of Genesis tells the story of the Tower of Babel, depicted here in a 16th-century painting by Pieter Bruegel the Elder. The Tower was a symbol of humanity's defiance against God, and the story was likely inspired by the great ziggurat temple of Babylon, where the Babylonian god Marduk was worshipped.

The Persian Empire

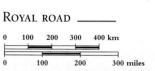

ROYAL ROAD _____

THE PERSIAN EMPIRE was vast. For 200 years its rule stretched from Greece to India, and from Egypt to Uzbekistan. The empire began in 550 BCE, when a young Persian king named Cyrus captured Ecbatana, the capital of the kingdom of Media. Cyrus then captured Lydia and finally, on 29 October 539 BCE, he captured Babylon, the greatest city in the world. Cyrus settled in Susa, his new capital. He divided his empire into 127 provinces, and established a realm-wide postal system so that the messengers could travel quickly across this vast empire. Cyrus allowed all the Israelites whom the Babylonians had captured to return home. So, with great joy, the Israelites made the 1,056-mile- (1,700-km-) long journey home on foot.

To speed up their postal system, the Persians built the Royal Road. It stretched from Sardis to Susa, about 1,550 miles (2,500 km).

1. The Temple is rebuilt
King Cyrus allowed the Jews to bring back to Jerusalem all the gold and silver treasures that the Babylonians had taken from the Temple. But now, there was no Temple to put them in—it had been destroyed by the Babylonians 50 years before. Encouraged by the prophets Haggai and Zechariah, the people laid foundations for a new, more humble Temple.

In 525 BCE the Persians added Egypt to their empire. Although the Egyptians were defeated, the Persians always feared that they might rebel.

4. Ezra and the Book of the Law
It took many years to rebuild Jerusalem after the Babylonian damage. Once the Temple and the city walls were finished, all the Israelites came to Jerusalem for a great celebration. Ezra, one of their leaders, read from the Book of the Law, which contained the commandments that God had given his people. The Israelites were filled with joy and worshipped God with all their hearts.

BLACK SEA

THRACE

MACEDONIA

LYDIA

● Athens

● Sardis

● Ephesus

CARIA

CILICIA

MEDITERRANEAN SEA

LIBYA

ABAR NAHARA

Damascus ●

● Jerusalem

● Memphis

SINAI

ARABIA

River Nile

EGYPT

RED SEA

3. Rebuilding the walls

Though people were living in Jerusalem again, the Persians would not permit them to build new city walls. They were afraid that the Egyptians might use Jerusalem as a base for rebellion. Finally, in 444 BCE, King Artaxerxes allowed his trusted servant Nehemiah, who was a Jew, to build new walls and gates.

Grand palace at Persepolis

Susa was the capital of the Persian Empire, but the Persian kings built magnificent new palaces at Persepolis. Here the kings sat in huge throne rooms, where musicians entertained them, great banquets were held, and gifts were brought to them from foreign kings.

Camels were ideal for long-distance travel, but only the wealthy could afford to travel this way.

Persian kings had their own special soldiers called "the immortals."

2. Esther's banquet

Life could be hard for the Jews in the Persian Empire. Haman, the chief minister, hated the Jews and persuaded King Ahasuerus to kill them all. However, Esther, the king's wife, was a Jew. At great risk, she invited the king and Haman to a banquet to reveal Haman's cruel plot. Then Haman had to beg for his own life.

Gold and silver poured into Susa and Persepolis. This was tribute, or payment, from lands across the empire.

The first Jewish exiles returned to Jerusalem in 538 BCE. Their journey was long and hard, but also joyful, because they were able to return to their homelands.

Alexander the Great

Alexander was one of the fiercest and cleverest Greek commanders of all time. In 334 BCE, he set out from Macedonia with his army and defeated the Persians in Lydia. The Persian king, Darius, led a huge army from Susa, and a fierce battle took place at Issus, but Darius lost. Alexander then marched south to conquer both Jerusalem and Egypt. Within three years the whole empire was Alexander's. The Persian Empire had ended and the Greek Empire had begun.

Map labels: CASPIAN SEA · SCYTHIA · Oxus River · ASSYRIA · PARTHIA · BACTRIA · Bactra · MEDIA · Nineveh · Ecbatana · Tigris River · BABYLONIA · Opis · Babylon · Susa · Nippur · Euphrates River · Persepolis · SHUSHAN · PERSIAN GULF

The New Testament

JESUS SPENT MUCH OF HIS LIFE in the towns and villages along the Sea of Galilee in northern Israel. The events leading up to his crucifixion and death took place further south in Jerusalem. Afterwards, the events of the New Testament moved beyond the Holy Land. The apostle Paul began his famous missionary journeys, traveling along the vast network of Roman roads, taking Jesus' message to Asia Minor and Greece before making the perilous sea journey to Rome.

Jesus enters Jerusalem
As Jesus rode into Jerusalem on a donkey, the people of Jerusalem waved palm branches and threw their coats down in his path. "Jesus is King!" they cried.

The Sea of Galilee, a large freshwater lake in northern Israel

Jesus' birth and early life

FIVE HUNDRED YEARS had passed since the Jews were allowed to return to Jerusalem. But they were still not free. In the 1st century BCE, the Holy Land (or Palestine) became part of the vast Roman Empire. The Jews had their own king, Herod the Great, but he only ruled with the permission of the Roman emperor Caesar Augustus, who was more than 1,200 miles (2,000 km) away in Rome. When Augustus wanted to know how much tax he could demand from Herod's kingdom, he ordered everybody to return to their family homes to be registered. It is at this time that the story of Jesus began. A young woman named Mary heard from the angel Gabriel that she was to be the mother of the Son of God. Just before the baby was due, Mary and her husband Joseph traveled 75 miles (120 km) from Nazareth in Galilee to Joseph's family home in Bethlehem to be registered. While they were in Bethlehem, Mary gave birth to a son, the baby Jesus.

1. The angel Gabriel visits Mary

Mary had just become engaged to Joseph, a young carpenter from Nazareth. One day, an angel named Gabriel suddenly appeared before her. Mary was terrified but the angel told her not to be afraid. "You are special! You have been chosen by God to be the mother of his son," the angel said. "But I'm a virgin," Mary replied. "How can I have a baby?" The angel told her that the Holy Spirit would make it happen, and that the child would be the Son of God. The baby was to be named Jesus, which means "savior." Mary was amazed, and said, "I will do whatever God wants."

2. The birth of Jesus

Bethlehem was crowded with people who had traveled there for the census. Mary and Joseph searched for a room to stay, but the only place they found was a stable. Jesus was born in the stable. Mary wrapped him in strips of cloth and laid him in a manger to keep him warm. On the night of his birth, in the fields above Bethlehem a group of angels told some shepherds about the birth of a savior. The shepherds hurried down from the hills to worship the baby Jesus.

Roman soldiers on the march were a common sight in Palestine, and the Romans kept an army in Jerusalem.

Many Roman officials worked for Herod. Some of them were involved in collecting taxes, which Herod had to pay to the Romans.

Jesus probably helped Joseph in his carpentry workshop. Here they made plows, carts, doors, and household tools.

Many people made a living by fishing on the Sea of Galilee. Nets constantly needed mending, and people spent many hours rebuilding them.

SEA OF GALILEE

Sidon

Tyre

Sepphoris • Nazareth

GALILEE

Dor

Caesarea

Scythopolis

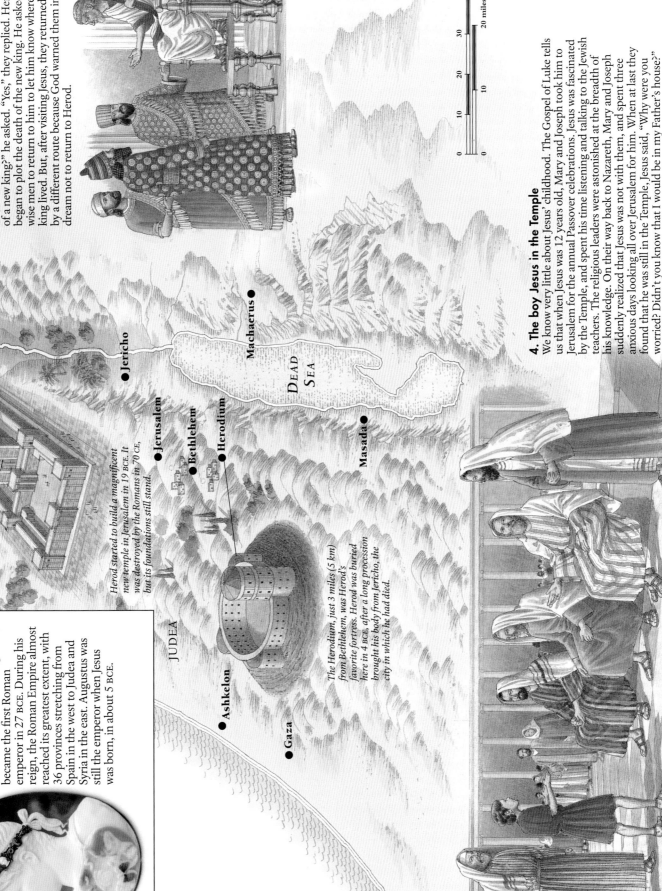

3. Herod meets the wise men

Everyone in Jerusalem was talking about the arrival of some men from the east dressed in rich clothing, who were following a bright star in the night sky. King Herod summoned them. "You say that the star means the birth of a new king?" he asked. "Yes," they replied. Herod began to plot the death of the new king. He asked the wise men to return to him to let him know where this king lived. But, after visiting Jesus, they returned home by a different route because God warned them in a dream not to return to Herod.

4. The boy Jesus in the Temple

We know very little about Jesus' childhood. The Gospel of Luke tells us that when Jesus was 12 years old, Mary and Joseph took him to Jerusalem for the annual Passover celebrations. Jesus was fascinated by the Temple, and spent his time listening and talking to the Jewish teachers. The religious leaders were astonished at the breadth of his knowledge. On their way back to Nazareth, Mary and Joseph suddenly realized that Jesus was not with them, and spent three anxious days looking all over Jerusalem for him. When at last they found that he was still in the Temple, Jesus said, "Why were you worried? Didn't you know that I would be in my Father's house?"

Caesar Augustus

Gaius Julius Caesar Octavianus, later known as Caesar Augustus, became the first Roman emperor in 27 BCE. During his reign, the Roman Empire almost reached its greatest extent, with 36 provinces stretching from Spain in the west to Judea and Syria in the east. Augustus was still the emperor when Jesus was born, in about 5 BCE.

Jordan River

SAMARIA

● Jericho

● Jerusalem
● Bethlehem
● Herodium

JUDEA

● Ashkelon

● Gaza

DEAD SEA

● Machaerus

● Masada

Herod started to build a magnificent new temple in Jerusalem in 19 BCE. It was destroyed by the Romans in 70 CE, but its foundations still stand.

The Herodium, just 3 miles (5 km) from Bethlehem, was Herod's favorite fortress. Herod was buried here in 4 BCE, after a long procession brought his body from Jericho, the city in which he had died.

40 km
20 miles
30
20
10
10
0
0

Mighty Masada

Between 37 and 31 BCE, King Herod the Great built the mighty fortress of Masada on a steep-sided, flat-topped hill near the Dead Sea. After the Romans conquered the region, they used the fortress to house their troops. In 66 CE, Masada was recaptured by Jewish resistance fighters. However, by 73 CE, it had been besieged by Roman legions, becoming the last Jewish fortress to fall to the Roman Empire.

Jesus begins his ministry

JESUS GREW UP IN NAZARETH, a small village in the hills of southern Galilee. He worked peacefully as a carpenter, helping his father Joseph. However, things were not so peaceful elsewhere. The Romans ruled the country, and feelings toward them were mixed in the Jewish community. Herod Antipas—the Roman-sponsored Jewish ruler of Galilee—and the Jewish aristocracy known as the Sadducees realized the benefits of keeping good relations with the Romans. Others, such as the Pharisees, resented the Romans and longed for God to save Israel from them. Some groups even attacked Roman soldiers, especially in Judea and Jerusalem. It was in this confused and dangerous situation that Jesus began to preach about the arrival of the Kingdom of God. When he was 30 years old, Jesus was baptized in the Jordan River, marking the beginning of his ministry. He traveled around Galilee with his chosen followers, known as the disciples, teaching in the synagogues, preaching on hillsides and beside the Sea of Galilee.

Galilee

The region of Galilee is situated to the west of a large lake called the Sea of Galilee (above). In Jesus' time, most people lived in the villages along the shore of the lake or in the rolling hills behind.

Temptations in the wilderness

After Jesus was baptized, the Spirit of God sent him alone into the desert to fast and pray for forty days. During this period, the devil visited Jesus and tried to persuade him to sin. However, Jesus resisted the devil's temptations, and obeyed God the Father.

Stones into bread
The devil tried to tempt Jesus to turn stones into bread. Although he was hungry, Jesus refused to use God's power for himself. He knew that he must rely entirely on God to meet his needs.

Falling from the temple
Next, the devil asked Jesus to jump off a high temple. The devil said that as the Son of God, Jesus would be protected by angels. Jesus again refused; he would not test God's power.

Kingdoms of the world
"You can have all this, if you worship me!" said the devil, showing Jesus the whole world from the top of a mountain. "No!" replied Jesus. "You must worship the Lord your God; serve him alone." After this final temptation, the devil disappeared and angels appeared to tend to Jesus.

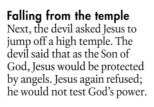

1. John baptizes Jesus
Huge crowds flocked from Jerusalem, Judea, and Galilee to hear the teachings of John the Baptist. They were excited, wondering whether John could be the Messiah— the "special Savior"—they were expecting. Jesus stood quietly among them, waiting to be baptized. When he saw Jesus, John exclaimed, "Look, the Lamb of God, who takes away the sin of the world!" After John had baptized Jesus, God's Holy Spirit came down in the form of a dove and settled on Jesus. God had publicly declared that Jesus was his beloved Son.

MEDITERRANEAN SEA

0	10	20	30 km
0	5	10	15	20 miles

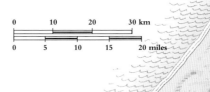

On every Sabbath day (Saturday) Jews would gather for worship in their synagogues.

Sidon

Tyre

Caesarea Philippi

Mount Hermon towers 9,232 ft (2,814 m) in the north of Israel. It is believed to be the place where the Transfiguration occurred.

SYRIA

Traditional houses in Galilee were made of mud brick, and had flat roofs. Crops, such as grapes, would often be dried on the roofs.

Capernaum
Cana
Magdala
Sepphoris **Tiberias**
Nazareth

SEA OF GALILEE

GALILEE

Nain

TETRARCHY OF PHILIP

DECAPOLIS

Jordan River

SAMARIA

Sychar

▲ *Mount Gerizim*

PERAEA

JUDEA

Jericho
Bethabara
Jerusalem

Bethlehem

WILDERNESS OF JUDEA

DEAD SEA

Machaerus

3. The Transfiguration

While in Caesarea Philippi, Jesus questioned his disciples. "Who do people say I am?" Jesus asked them. Peter rightly answered that Jesus was the Messiah, the Son of God. Six days later, Jesus took three of his disciples, Peter, James, and John, up to a mountain to pray. Suddenly, he began to glow brightly with God's glory. Moses and Elijah appeared beside Jesus, and spoke with him. The three disciples fell to the ground in fear. A bright cloud appeared, and the voice of God was heard saying, "This is my Son, whom I love. Listen to him!"

2. The wedding at Cana

One day Jesus and his mother Mary were invited to a wedding at Cana, in Galilee. When the wine ran out, Mary asked Jesus to help. Jesus told the waiting staff to fill six stone jars with water, and then serve it to the guests of the banquet. As the servers poured from these jars, they found that the water had turned into wine. The master of the banquet was amazed at the quality of the wine, which had miraculously appeared. This was Jesus' first miracle.

Machaerus was the site of one of Herod Antipas's fortresses. This is where John the Baptist was beheaded by Herod's soldiers.

The Pharisees were the leading teachers of the Torah (Jewish law and teaching). They were highly respected, and devoted their lives to studying.

Women in Galilee worked hard to keep the home clean and prepare meals for their family. They also worked in the fields at harvest time.

The miracles of Jesus

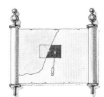

WHEN JESUS TURNED THE WATER into wine at the wedding in Cana, it was the start of a remarkable series of miracles. In particular, Jesus had wonderful healing power—he could heal people of any illness just by touching them and commanding the sickness or demons to leave. People from all over Galilee came to find him, bringing their sick relatives and friends. As Jesus' reputation spread, people came from even farther away—from Syria in the north, from Judea in the south, or from the Decapolis, the region east of the Sea of Galilee. Jesus traveled too, moving from town to town in Galilee with his disciples. Wherever he went he told people that his miracles were a sign of God's kingdom arriving among them. He encouraged people to turn to God with renewed faith, repenting of their sins. Because of these miracles, many Jews wondered if Jesus was the Messiah (the chosen deliverer of Israel) they had been waiting for to save them from the Romans.

Women made the daily bread. They mixed the dough on a flat stone, allowed it to rise, and then baked it over an open fire.

MEDITERRANEAN SEA

● **Ptolemais**

2. Feeding the five thousand

Many people followed Jesus and wanted to hear his teachings. One day, Jesus crossed to the eastern shore of Galilee by boat, hoping to rest, but a huge crowd still followed him by walking around the lake. Jesus taught them all day. By evening, everyone was hungry, and there was no food around. Jesus' disciples wanted him to rest, and asked him to send the crowds away. A small boy in the crowd had five loaves of bread and two small fishes. Jesus took this food from him, and after giving thanks to God, asked the disciples to pass around the pieces of bread and fish. The bread and fish had miraculously multiplied, and there was enough food to feed the five thousand people present.

The disciples of Jesus

Soon after he began his ministry, Jesus chose 12 special disciples. They were Simon Peter, Andrew, James, John, Philip, Bartholomew, Thomas, Matthew the tax collector, James, Thaddaeus, Simon the Zealot, and Judas Iscariot. The disciples lived, worked, and traveled with Jesus and witnessed his teaching. One of the disciples, Judas, would later go on to betray Jesus, leading to his arrest. After Jesus' death and resurrection, the remaining 11 disciples, along with a new disciple called Matthias, came to be known as the 12 apostles (meaning "sent ones"). They became the founders and leaders of the Christian Church. This 14th-century painting shows Jesus calling Simon Peter and Andrew to follow him.

Leprosy was a common disease at the time. People with leprosy had to live in a separate community and wear torn clothing to show that they were sufferers. Jesus cured a man with leprosy in Capernaum.

1. Jesus heals the paralyzed man

One day, in Capernaum, Jesus was teaching in a house packed with people. Four people arrived carrying a paralyzed man. They wanted Jesus to heal him, but could not make their way into the house. So they climbed onto the flat roof, stripped away the baked-earth covering, and lowered their friend down through the hole, right in front of Jesus. "Son," said Jesus, "your sins are forgiven." And then Jesus healed the man's paralysis. People were amazed when the man walked out, carrying his stretcher.

Jordan River

● Bethsaida

Capernaum ●

Gennesaret ●

Cana

Magdala ●

SEA OF GALILEE

Tiberias ●

Nazareth

3. Calming the storm

One day, Jesus and his disciples were crossing the Sea of Galilee when a huge storm blew up. Jesus was asleep in the stern, while Peter and the others desperately bailed water out of the boat. Eventually they woke him saying, "Teacher, help us!" Jesus stood up and spoke to the wind and water in a loud voice, "Peace! Be still!" The storm died down, and the disciples were amazed. "Why were you afraid?" Jesus asked them. "Have you no faith?" The disciples were in awe—even the winds obeyed his word.

Galilee was a wealthy area, because traders from the east passed through, sometimes bringing silk or spices for Rome.

4. Jairus' daughter

Jairus was the leader of the synagogue in one of the towns by the Sea of Galilee. When Jairus' 12-year-old daughter fell seriously ill, he rushed to find Jesus, saying, "Please, come before she dies!" But a messenger met them on the way, to say that the girl had died. "Don't be afraid!" Jesus said to Jairus. "Just have faith." When they reached Jairus' house, Jesus went in with Peter, James, and John, as well as Jairus and his wife. Jesus took the girl by the hand, and gently raised her back to life.

Jordan River

```
0    2    4    6    8 km

0        2        4        6 miles
```

Jesus travels to Jerusalem

JESUS SPENT MOST OF HIS MINISTRY in Galilee, but he occasionally traveled south to Jerusalem. All Jews attended the Temple in Jerusalem to celebrate the festivals—especially Passover (in March or April every year), the festival of Pentecost (or "Weeks," in May or June), and the festival of Tabernacles (in September or October). It was during his festival visits to Jerusalem, that Jesus became increasingly unpopular with religious leaders. On one visit he caused offense by healing a man on the Sabbath, a day when Jews are not supposed to work. On another, Jesus called himself the "light of the world," which deeply offended some of the Pharisees. They felt that Jesus was deceiving people with this bold claim. As the third Passover of his ministry drew near, Jesus knew that his enemies in Jerusalem were plotting to kill him. By now, news of Jesus' amazing ministry had spread far and wide. On this final journey to Jerusalem, Jesus traveled slowly, stopping often to teach and heal people. Jesus took a long route, first into Samaria, possibly to Ginae, and then down through the Jordan valley to Jericho. On the way, he told his disciples that he knew he would be arrested, tortured, and put to death in Jerusalem.

1. The good Samaritan

One day a Jewish lawyer asked Jesus who his neighbor was. In reply, Jesus told the tale of a man who had been robbed and left for dead on the side of a dangerous road from Jerusalem to Jericho. Both a priest and a Levite passed by the injured man without stopping to help him. But then a Samaritan stopped and cared for him. Jews and Samaritans hated one another, so in this story Jesus challenged the lawyer to expand his understanding of who his neighbor was. Jesus told him to go and be like the Samaritan.

Shepherds and their flocks did not stay in one place. They traveled around the countryside, looking for good grazing.

MEDITERRANEAN SEA

JESUS' FINAL JOURNEY TO JERUSALEM

```
0      5     10     15    20 km
|——|——|——|——|——|——|——|——|
0          5          10      15 miles
```

2. Zacchaeus the tax collector

In Jericho, huge crowds waited to see Jesus. The local tax collector was a wealthy, but much hated, man called Zacchaeus. He also longed to see Jesus, but had to climb a sycamore-fig tree beside the road to get a better view as he was very short. When Jesus arrived, he stopped under the tree and looked up. "Come down, Zacchaeus," he said, "I'd like to stay at your house." People were amazed that Jesus wanted to visit a man who was so disliked, but Zacchaeus was overwhelmed by Jesus' love. After supper, he declared that he would give half his possessions to the poor and repay anyone he had cheated. Jesus replied, "Today salvation has come to this house."

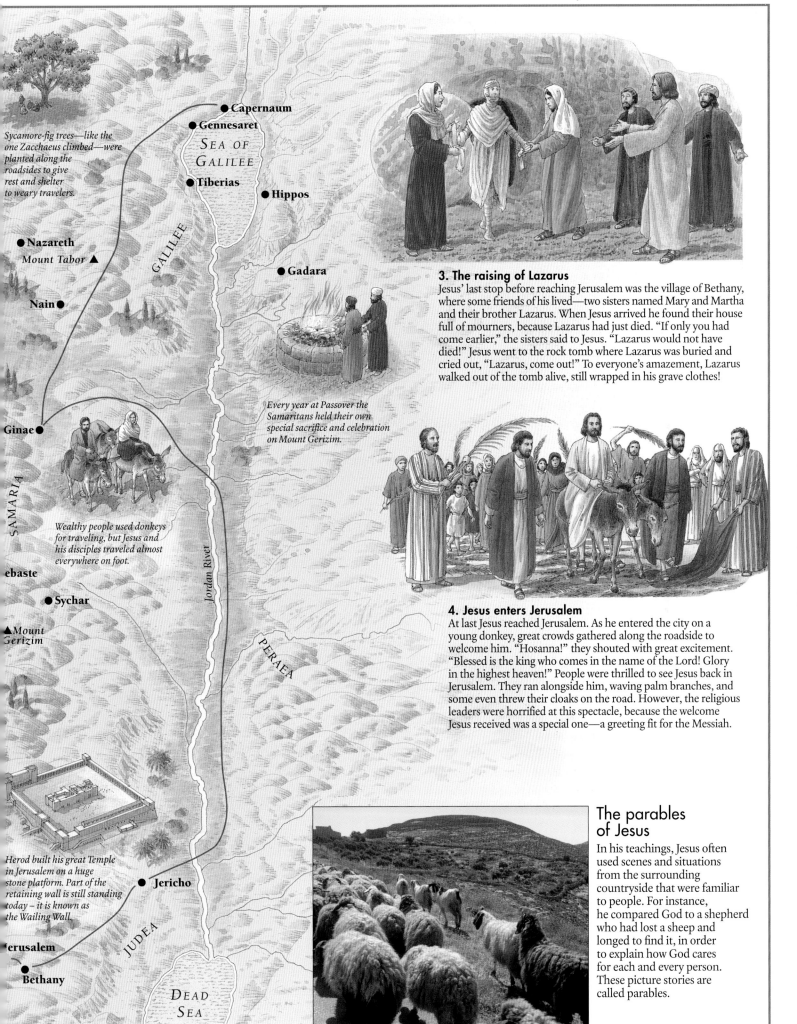

Sycamore-fig trees—like the one Zacchaeus climbed—were planted along the roadsides to give rest and shelter to weary travelers.

● **Capernaum**

● **Gennesaret**

SEA OF
GALILEE

● **Tiberias**

● **Hippos**

● **Nazareth**

Mount Tabor ▲

Nain ●

GALILEE

● **Gadara**

Every year at Passover the Samaritans held their own special sacrifice and celebration on Mount Gerizim.

Ginae ●

Wealthy people used donkeys for traveling, but Jesus and his disciples traveled almost everywhere on foot.

SAMARIA

ebaste

● **Sychar**

▲ *Mount Gerizim*

Jordan River

PERAEA

3. The raising of Lazarus

Jesus' last stop before reaching Jerusalem was the village of Bethany, where some friends of his lived—two sisters named Mary and Martha and their brother Lazarus. When Jesus arrived he found their house full of mourners, because Lazarus had just died. "If only you had come earlier," the sisters said to Jesus. "Lazarus would not have died!" Jesus went to the rock tomb where Lazarus was buried and cried out, "Lazarus, come out!" To everyone's amazement, Lazarus walked out of the tomb alive, still wrapped in his grave clothes!

4. Jesus enters Jerusalem

At last Jesus reached Jerusalem. As he entered the city on a young donkey, great crowds gathered along the roadside to welcome him. "Hosanna!" they shouted with great excitement. "Blessed is the king who comes in the name of the Lord! Glory in the highest heaven!" People were thrilled to see Jesus back in Jerusalem. They ran alongside him, waving palm branches, and some even threw their cloaks on the road. However, the religious leaders were horrified at this spectacle, because the welcome Jesus received was a special one—a greeting fit for the Messiah.

Herod built his great Temple in Jerusalem on a huge stone platform. Part of the retaining wall is still standing today – it is known as the Wailing Wall

● **Jericho**

JUDEA

'erusalem

● **Bethany**

DEAD
SEA

The parables of Jesus

In his teachings, Jesus often used scenes and situations from the surrounding countryside that were familiar to people. For instance, he compared God to a shepherd who had lost a sheep and longed to find it, in order to explain how God cares for each and every person. These picture stories are called parables.

Jesus clears the Temple

The Temple was the most important building in Jerusalem, and the center of Jewish religious life. In its courtyard, people could change their money into special Temple coinage in order to buy animals for sacrifices. When Jesus arrived at the Temple, he interrupted this business by overturning the tables of the money-changers, as masterfully captured in this 14th-century painting by Italian artist Giotto. Jesus did this to let people know that access to God did not need to be bought, but was available freely through Jesus himself.

Jesus' death and resurrection

AT THE END OF THEIR LONG JOURNEY, Jesus and his disciples stood on the Mount of Olives and looked across the Kidron valley at Jerusalem. Much of this beautiful city had been rebuilt during the time of Herod the Great (37–4 BCE), and by the time of Jesus' last visit, Jerusalem was one of the grandest cities in Rome's eastern empire. However, on his arrival Jesus was filled with deep sadness—he knew that as soon as the Passover festival ended, he would be arrested and killed. Jesus had made many enemies since his arrival in Jerusalem—Jewish leaders felt that his increasing popularity threatened them and the fragile power balance with Rome. Jesus spent Passover in Jerusalem with his 12 disciples, and told them that one among them would betray him. After this last supper, Jesus and the disciples went to the Garden of Gethsemane, situated on the side of the Mount of Olives, to pray and rest. While the disciples slept, Jesus prayed to God the Father to give him strength to go through the ordeal he knew he had soon to face.

Jesus' body was laid in a tomb like this, with a large, round stone forming the entrance that could be rolled aside.

Damascus Gate

Golgotha, where Jesus was crucified

Special spices were used to prepare bodies for burial. Ointments were made and then sealed onto the body with bandages.

1. The betrayal
Jesus finished his prayers late in the evening and eventually returned to his disciples, who were sleeping in the olive grove. Suddenly Judas, one of Jesus' disciples appeared with a crowd carrying swords and burning torches. Judas went up to Jesus and said, "Master!" and gave him a kiss on the cheek. This was a signal to the crowd, and immediately two men came forward and seized Jesus to arrest him. Judas had been paid thirty pieces of silver by the chief priests for betraying Jesus.

Herod's Palace

2. The trial of Jesus
Jesus was taken to a Jewish court and quickly condemned to die for claiming to be the Son of God. Next, he was taken to Pilate, the Roman governor, because only Romans could authorize executions. Jesus' enemies stood outside, shouting for his crucifixion. Pilate addressed the crowd, telling them that in his view Jesus was innocent. But the crowd shouted so loudly that Pilate gave in to their demand. He washed his hands in front of the crowds, to show that he wanted no part in Jesus' death.

Area where the Last Supper is supposed to have taken place

| 0 | 100 | 200 | 300 m |

| 0 | 100 | 200 | 300 yards |

City walls

3. The crucifixion

Jesus was stripped of his clothing, dressed in a scarlet robe, and mocked by Roman soldiers who called him "king of the Jews." A crown of thorns was forced upon his head, and after being beaten, Jesus was made to carry his cross through the streets of Jerusalem to Golgotha. Before noon, Jesus was nailed to the cross and crucified alongside two criminals. Onlookers shouted insults, but Jesus said, "Father, forgive them, for they do not know what they do." From about noon to 3 o'clock, darkness descended over the land. Then Jesus cried out, "Father, into your hands I commend my spirit," and he breathed his last. Looking on, a Roman centurion exclaimed, "Surely this man was the Son of God!"

The Passover meal was one of the highlights of the year. Jewish families gathered to remember the night when the Israelites left Egypt for the Promised Land.

Herod's Temple, where religious leaders questioned Jesus

The Mount of Olives, just to the east of Jerusalem, gave a wonderful view of the city to travelers arriving from Jericho.

KIDRON VALLEY

Court of the Gentiles

Pool of Siloam

4. The road to Emmaus

Two days after Jesus' death, two of his disciples were traveling to Emmaus, a village near Jerusalem. Suddenly a stranger joined them, and asked them why they looked so sad. They told him about Jesus and their lost hopes. To their surprise the stranger said, "Haven't you read your Scriptures? The Messiah had to suffer, but he'll rise again!" At the end of their journey, the two disciples realized that the stranger was Jesus—and rushed to Jerusalem to tell the other disciples that they had seen Jesus alive.

5. The ascension

Over a period of six weeks, Jesus appeared to the disciples several times in Jerusalem and in Galilee. He told them that they must spread the message of God's kingdom, and that God would give them power to do this by sending his Holy Spirit to them. Finally, Jesus led the disciples to a mountain in Galilee. "All authority in heaven and on earth has been given to me," he said. "Go and make disciples of all nations, baptizing them. And surely I am with you always." Then he was taken from them in a cloud. As the disciples watched, two men dressed in white appeared and told them that Jesus would one day return in the same way.

The resurrection

The moment of Jesus' resurrection is not described in the Bible. The Gospels only tell us that Jesus' body was placed in a sealed tomb, which was found to be open and empty on the morning of the third day. Different artists through the centuries have depicted the moment of resurrection in their own ways, often using images from their context to show the surprise of encountering the risen Jesus. In this 15th-century work by Italian artist Andrea Mantegna, Jesus rises from a sarcophagus instead of emerging from a tomb.

The Early Church

BEFORE HE ASCENDED TO HEAVEN, Jesus gave his disciples a promise. "When the Holy Spirit has come upon you, you will receive power and will tell people about me everywhere in Jerusalem, throughout Judea, in Samaria, and to the ends of the Earth." The disciples received the Holy Spirit on the day of Pentecost, and boldly began to speak about Jesus all over Jerusalem. Many people were convinced when they heard about Jesus' resurrection. The message spread quickly, and soon there were thousands of Jews who believed that Jesus was the true Messiah. Some Jews, however, were horrified, particularly those who had been Jesus' enemies. They began to arrest Jesus' followers and even killed some of them. One of these opponents was a Pharisee named Saul. He hated the followers of the Way, as the early Christians were often called. However, when Jesus appeared to him, Saul was transformed into a fearless missionary on his behalf. Based in the church at Antioch in Syria, Saul made several missionary journeys spreading the word of Jesus. He became known by his Roman name, Paul, because he was one of the first to bring the Christian message to non-Jewish people.

The whole Roman Empire was crisscrossed by excellent roads, which made traveling much easier for the first Christian missionaries.

PAUL'S JOURNEY TO DAMASCUS _____
PAUL'S FIRST JOURNEY 45 CE _____
PAUL'S SECOND JOURNEY 50 CE _____
PAUL'S THIRD JOURNEY 55 CE _____
PAUL'S JOURNEY TO ROME 60 CE _____

0   50   100   150   200   250 km
0   50   100   150 miles

4. Paul's shipwreck

On his journeys, Paul had made many enemies who wanted him to be arrested and executed. Eventually, Paul was taken as a prisoner to Rome to appear before the emperor, Nero. On the sea journey to Rome, disaster struck. A great north-easterly wind blew up, and the ship was driven helplessly for fourteen days until it reached the coast of Malta. God assured Paul that no lives would be lost, and all 276 people on board got safely to shore.

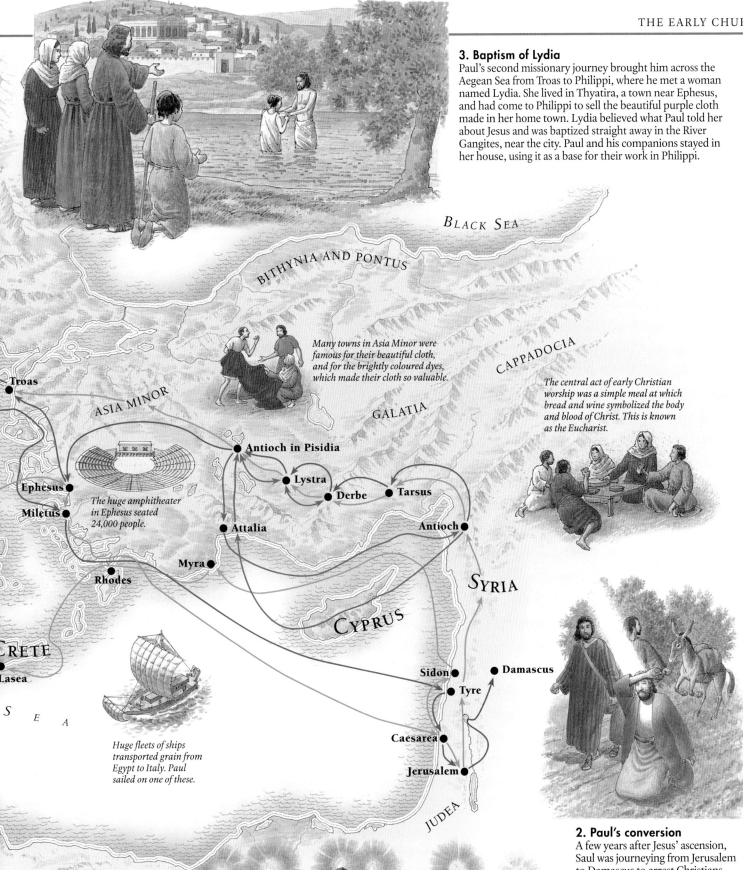

3. Baptism of Lydia

Paul's second missionary journey brought him across the Aegean Sea from Troas to Philippi, where he met a woman named Lydia. She lived in Thyatira, a town near Ephesus, and had come to Philippi to sell the beautiful purple cloth made in her home town. Lydia believed what Paul told her about Jesus and was baptized straight away in the River Gangites, near the city. Paul and his companions stayed in her house, using it as a base for their work in Philippi.

Many towns in Asia Minor were famous for their beautiful cloth, and for the brightly coloured dyes, which made their cloth so valuable.

The central act of early Christian worship was a simple meal at which bread and wine symbolized the body and blood of Christ. This is known as the Eucharist.

The huge amphitheater in Ephesus seated 24,000 people.

Huge fleets of ships transported grain from Egypt to Italy. Paul sailed on one of these.

BLACK SEA

BITHYNIA AND PONTUS

CAPPADOCIA

ASIA MINOR

GALATIA

Troas

Ephesus

Miletus

Antioch in Pisidia

Lystra

Derbe

Tarsus

Attalia

Antioch

Myra

SYRIA

Rhodes

CYPRUS

CRETE

Lasea

S E A

Sidon

Damascus

Tyre

Caesarea

Jerusalem

JUDEA

2. Paul's conversion

A few years after Jesus' ascension, Saul was journeying from Jerusalem to Damascus to arrest Christians. However, just outside Damascus a bright light suddenly flashed, and Saul heard a voice: "Saul, Saul, why are you persecuting me?" "Who are you, Lord?" Saul asked. "I am Jesus, the one you are persecuting!" the voice answered. "Now get up and go into Damascus. You will be told what you are to do." Saul became a Christian, and one of the greatest missionaries and thinkers of the Christian Church.

1. Tongues of fire

Shortly after the ascension, Jesus' disciples gathered in a room in Jerusalem to celebrate the Jewish festival of Pentecost. Suddenly they heard a great wind, and tongues of fire appeared among them. It was the sign of the Holy Spirit, and the disciples began to speak in different languages. People from many other countries had come to Jerusalem for the festival, and were amazed when the disciples began to speak to them about God's mighty acts in their own language.

A–Z of Bible places

THE EVENTS OF THE BIBLE MOSTLY TAKE PLACE in the Middle East. After the early stories of creation, the Bible's story focuses on Abraham, who was born in Ur, in present-day Iraq. It ends nearly 2,000 years later with Paul, one of the greatest Christian apostles, in Rome, the capital of the Roman Empire. In the 2,175 miles (3,500 km) between Ur and Rome lie Syria, Lebanon, Turkey, Israel, and Greece, with Egypt to the south. This is where the story is set, focused around the land of Israel and the ancient city of Jerusalem. Listed here are some of the main places mentioned in the Bible.

Ammon
A country to the east of the Dead Sea. The Israelites passed through Ammon on their way to the Promised Land.

Antioch
This city in Syria was one of the largest cities in the world at the time of Jesus. It was the place where followers of Jesus were first called "Christians."

Ashdod
One of the five chief cities of the Philistines. Ashdod was the biggest, with its own port nearby and a huge statue of the god Dagon.

Ashkelon
Another Philistine city, on the coast between Jaffa and Gaza. King Herod the Great was born here.

Assyria
An ancient kingdom east of the Holy Land that became a mighty empire in the 8th and 7th centuries BCE. The Assyrian armies captured the northern kingdom of Israel in 724 BCE and carried many people into exile from their homes.

Athens
The capital and chief city of Greece. Paul preached a famous sermon here.

Attalia
The chief port of Pamphylia, on the southern coast of Asia Minor.

Babel
The name of the earliest city on the site of Babylon. Here people tried to build a massive tower up to heaven.

Babylon
A city on the River Euphrates, 80 km (49 miles) south of Baghdad. It became very powerful as the centre of a huge empire. Babylon was most famous for its fabled hanging gardens, which King Nebuchadnezzar built for his wife, Amytis.

Beersheba
An important town about 75 km (46 miles) south-west of Jerusalem. It existed in the time of Abraham and is often referred to as one of the southernmost towns in Israel.

Bethany
A village on the other side of the Mount of Olives, 3 km (1.8 miles) from Jerusalem.

Bethel
Bethel is the Hebrew word for "House of God," and the name reminded people that God had appeared to Jacob in a dream he had here. Later, Bethel became a religious center.

Bethlehem
Just 5.5 miles (9 km) south of Jerusalem, Bethlehem is the birthplace of both King David and Jesus.

Bethsaida
A village at the northern end of the Sea of Galilee, which Jesus often visited. Three of his disciples—Peter, Andrew, and Philip—came from here.

Caesarea Philippi
A town in the far north, nestled at the foot of Mount Hermon. Herod's son Philip, who ruled this area, called it Caesarea after Roman emperor Caesar Augustus.

Cana
The village in Galilee where Jesus performed his first miracle—turning water into wine.

Canaan
The name of the land of Israel before the Israelite tribes entered it after their long journey from Egypt. This land was promised to the Israelites from God.

Capernaum
Jesus made this town his base of operations. It was situated on the densely populated western shore of the Sea of Galilee.

Carmel
The mountain range to the northeast of Galilee, situated near the Mediterranean coast. Here, Elijah challenged the prophets of the god Baal.

Colossae
Paul wrote one of his New Testament letters to the church in this little town, which was up the valley of the River Lycus, not far from Ephesus.

Corinth
One of the chief cities of Greece. It was a very busy trading city, home to people from all over the Mediterranean. Paul lived here for nearly two years, preaching about Jesus and founding a church.

Damascus
The chief city of Syria in New Testament times and today. It is a very old city, and is mentioned throughout the Bible. Paul became a follower of Jesus on the road to Damascus, and then had to escape from the city by being lowered from the city wall in a basket.

Dead Sea
A lake between Israel and Jordan, the surface of which is the lowest place on earth— 1,412 ft (431 m) below sea level.

Decapolis
Meaning ten cities, it is a region to the east of Galilee and the Jordan River where Jesus ministered.

Dothan
A town south of Mount Carmel. Here, Joseph's brothers sold him to Ishmaelite traders on their way to Egypt.

Edom
The country south of the Dead Sea. It belonged to Israel under David and Solomon, but later became independent.

Egypt
Large country in the northeast corner of Africa. Ninety-six percent of Egypt is desert and nearly all its people live in the four percent of habitable land, on both sides of the Nile River. The Israelites lived there until the Exodus, under Moses' leadership.

Ekron
One of the five great Philistine cities. It was only 22 miles (35 km) west of Jerusalem, so the Israelites often felt threatened, having enemies living so close to them.

En Gedi
An important oasis and freshwater spring west of the Dead Sea. David hid there when he was running from Saul.

Ephesus
One of the biggest cities in the world in the time of Paul, who spent over two years there preaching about Jesus.

Euphrates
The longest river in western Asia, sometimes just called "the river" in the Bible. The Holy Land was part of the Persian province called "Beyond the River"—that is, west of the Euphrates.

Galatia
The area in southern Asia Minor that Paul and Barnabas visited on their first missionary journey.

Galilee
A lake and a region in northern Israel. Jesus grew up here and spent much of his ministry in the many towns and cities of this region. The Sea of Galilee (actually a lake) is mentioned in many of the Gospel stories in the Bible.

Gath
One of the five Philistine cities. The giant Goliath, whom David killed with a stone, came from Gath.

Gethsemane
The garden on the side of the Mount of Olives where Jesus prayed on the night he was betrayed and arrested.

Gilboa
The mountain in the territory of Issachar, in north Israel, where King Saul and his sons were killed by the Philistines.

Gilead
A large area east of the Jordan valley, extending north of the Dead Sea where the tribes of Reuben, Gad, and Manasseh settled.

Goshen
The fertile area in the Nile Delta where the Israelites lived during their time in Egypt. Goshen was saved from the plagues suffered by the rest of Egypt just before the Exodus.

Greece
Following the victories of the Greek king Alexander the Great, Greece supplied a common language and culture to the whole of the eastern Mediterranean, including Israel.

Haran
A town in present-day southeast Turkey. Abraham lived in Haran before moving south into Canaan.

Hazor
This northern city was the largest Canaanite city when Joshua and the Israelites conquered the land. Hazor was destroyed by the Assyrians in the 8th century BCE.

Hebron

The highest town in the Holy Land, Hebron was just 19 miles (30 km) from Jerusalem. Here, Abraham, Isaac, and Jacob were buried, and King David began his reign here—it was his capital before he captured Jerusalem.

Hermon

This great mountain north of Galilee, rising to 9,232 ft (2,814 m), separates Israel from Syria. Jesus' Transfiguration may have taken place here.

Israel

The country and the nation at the heart of the Bible. Sometimes this name is used for the whole people, sometimes just for the ten-tribe northern kingdom.

Jericho

A town west of the Jordan River, Jericho was the first great walled city of Canaan, conquered by Joshua and the Israelites. It is one of the oldest cities in the world.

Jerusalem

The capital of Israel since about 1000 BCE, when King David settled there and united the nation. Since that time, Jerusalem became the holy city for the Jews, and later for the Christians and the Muslims. The name means "city of peace," but it has often been surrounded by war.

Jordan

The Jordan River rises in the north on Mount Hermon, fed by the snow there, and flows down the Jordan valley to the Dead Sea.

Judea

This was the Greek and Roman name for the Holy Land. In the time of Paul the Roman province of Judea included Judah and Jerusalem in the south, Samaria, and Galilee. The "Wilderness of Judea" mentioned in reference to John the Baptist is the desert west of the Dead Sea.

Lachish

A large Canaanite town, 30 miles (48 km) southwest of Jerusalem, taken over by the Israelites. It was turned into a fort, but later captured by the Assyrians.

Lystra

A remote city in the Roman province of Galatia (near Konya in Turkey). Paul and Barnabas visited this town on their first missionary journey. Here, Paul healed a crippled man, but was stoned and nearly killed. Some of the people of Lystra became Christians and Paul returned to visit.

Macedonia

The kingdom in northern Greece from which King Alexander the Great came. Paul dreamed about a man asking him to come to Macedonia and help them. Paul made the visit on his second missionary journey.

Masada

The fortress near the Dead Sea where the Jews held out against the Roman army in 73 CE.

Megiddo

A large ancient city near Mount Carmel. The Canaanite king of Megiddo was defeated by Joshua when the Israelites conquered Canaan. Later, King Josiah died there, fighting the Egyptians. During his reign, Solomon chose it as one of his fortified towns.

Mesopotamia

This Greek name means "between the rivers." It describes the ancient area between the Tigris and Euphrates, which contained some of the world's oldest cities, including Babylon, Nineveh, and Ur, Abraham's birthplace.

Midian

The Midianites were nomadic people who lived south of Israel, way down in the Sinai Peninsula. They were famous for the camels they bred. Moses' wife, Zipporah, was a Midianite.

Moab

Moab was the country situated on a high plateau of land east of the Dead Sea. The Moabites were often enemies of Israel, but the book of Ruth tells the story of how a Moabite girl came to live in Bethlehem.

Nain

The village in Galilee where Jesus stopped a funeral procession and brought a young man back to life.

Nazareth

The town in Galilee where Jesus grew up and worked with his father, Joseph, as a carpenter.

Nile

The Nile River flows from Lake Victoria, in Tanzania, 3,480 miles (5,600 km) south of the Mediterranean. It gives life to Egypt, supplying water to grow crops in the desert. Its water turned to blood in one of the ten plagues that took place before the Exodus.

Nimrud

Nimrud is the modern name of the ancient city of Calah, or Kalhu, one of the chief cities of the Assyrian Empire. It lay beside the Tigris River, just south of Nineveh.

Nineveh

The capital of Assyria, and of the Assyrian Empire, built beside the Tigris River in what is now northern Iraq. Nineveh was a powerful city, but fell to the Babylonians in 612 BCE, as predicted by the prophet Zephaniah. The site of the city goes back to about 4500 BCE.

Persia

Cyrus, king of Persia (present-day Iran), conquered the Babylonians in 540 BCE, and the Persian Empire then grew until it was the largest empire the world had ever seen. The empire was divided into 127 provinces, and great roads were built to hold the empire together. It was King Cyrus who allowed exiled Jews to return to their homelands.

Philippi

A large town, and also a Roman colony, on the coast of Macedonia, where many retired Roman soldiers lived. Paul visited Philippi as part of his mission.

Philistia

The country of the Philistines. It was on the coastal strip west of Judah and the Dead Sea, and centered on the Philistines' five chief cities: Ashkelon, Gaza, Ashdod, Gath, and Ekron.

Qumran

An area near the Dead Sea, famous for the discovery of the Dead Sea scrolls found there. These scrolls provide a picture of Jewish religious life and writings in the first century CE.

Red Sea

The arm of the sea that separates Egypt and northeast Africa from Arabia. In the Bible it is sometimes called the "Reed Sea."

Rome

The capital of the Roman Empire in Italy. Roman armies first invaded the Holy Land in 63 BCE, and from then onward the country was ruled by Rome—either directly, by governors like Pilate, or indirectly, through the Herods. Jews generally hated Roman rule.

Samaria

Capital of the Northern Kingdom of Israel, built by King Omri to rival Jerusalem. His son King Ahab continued the building. Samaria fell to the Assyrians in 721 BCE and it was later rebuilt by King Herod, who renamed it Sebaste.

Sheba

The kingdom of Sheba is thought have been located in present-day Yemen or Ethiopia. In the 10th century BCE, the Queen of Sheba visited King Solomon to test his wisdom.

Shechem

An ancient town in central Israel, about 31 miles (50 km) north of Jerusalem. Abraham stayed in Shechem, Joshua gathered all the tribes of Israel here, and later, the northern tribes rejected King Rehoboam here.

Sidon

Originally founded by the Phoenicians to provide a harbor on the north coast of the Holy Land (today it is in Lebanon). It is mentioned throughout the Bible—Jezebel was the daughter of the king of Sidon, and Jesus visited Sidon and its neighboring city of Tyre in the New Testament.

Sinai

The mountain in Arabia where God gave the Law to Moses. Unfortunately, we do not know for sure which mountain this was. It is also the name of a desert and a peninsula.

Susa

One of the great cities of the Persian Empire. Darius I built a lavish palace here, the remains of which can still be seen today.

Tarsus

The city near the coast of Cilicia (southern Turkey) where Paul was born. He called it "no ordinary city."

Thessalonica

The chief city of Macedonia (northern Greece). Here, Paul preached on his second missionary journey, and wrote two of his New Testament letters to the church.

Tiberias

Herod Antipas built the city of Tiberias, on the western shore of the Sea of Galilee, to be his capital. He named it after the Roman emperor Tiberius.

Tyre

A large port situated 25 miles (40 km) south of Sidon. King Hiram of Tyre supplied many of the materials for Solomon's Temple in Jerusalem. In New Testament times, Jesus visited and preached in Tyre.

Ur

This city in ancient Mesopotamia or Chaldea (now southern Iraq) is famous for its ziggurat (a rectangular temple tower). It is the birthplace of Abraham.

Index

Biblical references are added in italics so that you can read more about your favorite stories and places in the Bible.

Acknowledgments

The publisher would like to thank the following people for their help with making this book:
Julia Harris, Peter Radcliffe, Tanvi Sahu, and Vicky Wharton for design assistance; Vandana Likhmania, Scarlett O'Hara, Rupa Rao, and Martin Redfern for editorial assistance; Mollie Gillard, Sally Hamilton, Rachel Hilford, and Amanda Russell for additional picture research; Michelle Baxter and Lindsey Kent for assistance with the second edition; Simon Mumford for map consultancy; Suhita Dharamjit and Saloni Singh for the jacket; Hazel Beynon for proofreading; and Chris Bernstein for the index. Many thanks also to Rupert Chapman and Felicity Cobbing at the Palestine Exploration Fund.

The publisher would like to thank the following for their kind permission to reproduce their photographs:
(Key: a–above; b–below/bottom; c–center; f–far; l–left; r–right; t–top)

123RF.com: Sofia Potanina 16ca. Alamy Stock Photo: Albatross / Duby Tal 14–15, Album 54–55, Bible Land Pictures / Zev Radovan 5crb, 6crb, 8br, 8–9c, 25bl, 28–29, 53bc, Carlos Espina 41tr, Eddie Gerald 32–33, IanDagnall Computing 50bc, Lanmas 13cra, 30tr, mauritius images GmbH / Steve Vidler 45bl, robertharding / Victoria Theakston 6bc, Stockimo / stevenjamesgallery 48tr, Rosanne Tackaberry 42–43, The Art Archive / Gianni Dagli Orti 18–19. Bridgeman Images: English School 26bl, Andrea Mantegna 58–59, Pieter the Elder 38–39. © The Trustees of the British Museum. All rights reserved: 8c. Dorling Kindersley: Alan Hills / Barbara Winter © The Trustees of the British Museum All rights reserved. 9bl, 9bc. Dreamstime.com: Compuinfoto 9br, Mindaugas Dulinskas 46–47, Anna Zolnay 6clb. Getty Images: Dea Picture Library / De Agostini Editorial 4–5, Maremagnum 7clb, Moment / Anton Petrus 10–11, Sygma / Jeffrey Markowitz 8bl, Universal History Archive 36tc. Getty Images / iStock: Joel Carillet 21cra, Jupiterimages 30cl, oversnap 37cra. Palestine Exploration Fund: Reproduced by kind permission of the Palestine Exploration Fund 9tr.

All other images © Dorling Kindersley

64

WHAT WILL YOU DISCOVER NEXT?

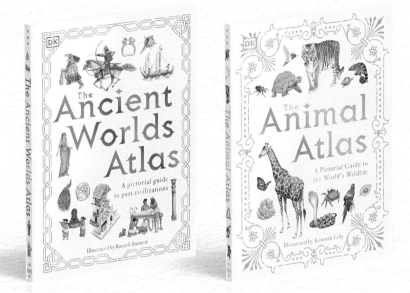

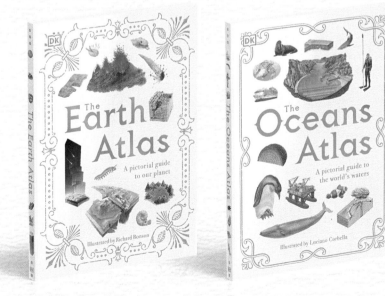